COMMUNITY

THE TIE THAT BINDS

Mary F. Rousseau

UNIVERSITY
PRESS OF
AMERICA

Lanham, New York, London

Copyright © 1991 by
University Press of America®, Inc.
4720 Boston Way
Lanham, Maryland 20706

3 Henrietta Street
London WC2E 8LU England

Library of Congress Cataloging-in-Publication Data

Rousseau, Mary F.
Community : the tie that binds / Mary F. Rousseau.
p.   cm.
Includes bibliographical references.
1. Community.   2. Social values.
3. Conduct of life.   I. Title.
HM131.R814 1991
303.3'72—dc20   91–7430 CIP

ISBN 0–8191–8209–5 (cloth)
ISBN 0–8191–8210–9 (paper)

The paper used in this publication meets the minimum requirements of
American National Standard for Information Sciences—Permanence
of Paper for Printed Library Materials, ANSI Z39.48–1984.

Dedication: To all with whom I have studied philosophy,

"And so, too, it seems, should one make a return to those with whom one has studied philosophy; for their worth cannot be measured against money, and they can get no honors which will balance their services; but still it is perhaps enough, as it is with the gods and one's parents, to give them what one can."

Nichomachean Ethics, IX, 1, 1164b 2-6.

Table of Contents

PREFACE

This book seeks to articulate, in a systematic way, the "second language" referred to by the authors of *Habits of the Heart*.[1] Robert Bellah and his colleagues present a penetrating and detailed analysis of the "first language" of contemporary Americans, the language of individualism. They also refer to a dormant and fragmentary language, a "second language" persistent throughout our history, the language of community. Each of these languages is a cluster not only of words, but of thought patterns and behaviors through which we Americans seek, find and express our personal identities, our sense of meaning and fulfillment for our lives. In the predominant "first language" of individualism, persons are seen as detached, even competitive centers of rights and freedom. We are free to define our rights as we see fit and to pursue them, subject only to the restraints negotiated with other free individuals seeking their idiosyncratically defined rights. In the "second language" of community, persons are seen as innately connected to each other, naturally cooperative in pursuing a fulfillment dictated by the traits of our common human nature and dignity. This "second language," obvious in the Biblical and republican traditions of our early history, has not survived the industrialization of our society except in fragmentary form, in large part below the level of fully conscious thought, whether private or public. Bellah *et al.* see individualism as a serious threat to our existence as a free people, and call for a revival of community as our best, perhaps only, hope.

This book differs, however, from other recent and important treatises on community. It is a systematic *philosophical* exposition of the presuppositions of social, political, psychological and theological theories which value community as an essential human good. It presents a view of the nature of persons, of human fulfillment and human associations, of the rights and wrongs of human behavior, as these affect the building of community. It thus makes explicit some important assumptions that are present but only implicitly, and often incoherently, in the writings of contemporary social thinkers, both individualist and communal. Like *Habits of*

---

[1] Bellah, Robert, Richard Madsen, William Sullivan, Ann Swidler, and Steven Tipton, *Habits of the Heart: Individualism and Commitment in American Life* (Berkeley, University of California Press, 1985).

the Heart, this book is a normative treatise, seeing community as a necessary good, as a standard for our behavior, as
the right way for human beings to live. It is, indeed, an ethical treatise – but ethical at one remove from *Habits of the
Heart*. Bellah *et al.* call for a cultural transformation that
would revive the virtues that enable us to pursue the public
good rather than a conglomerate of private goods. That cultural transformation is no small matter: it calls for a reversal
of the basic drive of our culture, the urge toward economic
success. It would turn us toward a social ecology in which we
would value, and cultivate, the ties that bind us together in
pursuit of a common personal good. And certain behaviors,
certain habits of the heart, would be good or evil, ethically
right or wrong, as means toward or away from that common
good.

The social ecology that Bellah and company recommend
as the goal of our common pursuit is not money and the
things that money can buy, but a set of immaterial and in-
tangible goods that are distinctively the work of human beings. It calls for a reform of work into an activity that is
intrinsically, not just economically, valuable – a way of using
one's special talents, of enjoying approval of and fellowship
with others, and of combining one's work with full participation in family life. They call for the development of culture
as the outward symbolizing of ideas and feelings, enjoyed for
its own sake. They call for a psychological change as well
– not just the raising of consciousness to an appreciation of
what is distinctively human, but a conversion of our motivation away from self-seeking and toward altruism. This last
change would enable us to transcend our own egoism, so that
we would generate true romance and friendship, and create
and enjoy beautiful surroundings. In short, their new set of
"habits of the heart" would lead us to "practices of life, good
in themselves, that are inherently fulfilling."[2]

This book offers an articulation of this "second language"
in a fairly complete and systematic way, and more. It goes
beyond ethics to the metaphysical roots of our moral life.
It offers, in the technical sense of the term, a *philosophy* of
community – not a linguistics, nor a sociology, not a psychology, nor a politics of community, but a philosophy. As such
a philosophy, a metaphysics in which an ethics is rooted, it

---

[2] *Habits of the Heart*, p. 295.

asks the deepest question underlying any inquiry into community. What precisely is the tie that binds, the tie that binds in both senses of the word? What is the tie that binds us existentially, that makes us truly one in our very being? And why and how does that tie bind us morally? How does it direct us, indeed oblige us, to seek or to avoid certain interactions with each other? In seeking that existential tie, we are seeking the roots of moral obligation. Bellah *et al.* are motivated by a concern that is ultimately pragmatic, the continuing existence of our nation as free rather than totalitarian. But such a project does not reach the deepest roots of moral concern. Why is a free society better than a totalitarian one? Does it deserve to exist simply because it is free? Is the altruistic enjoyment of culture, of family life, of dignified and enjoyable work an end in itself? In other words, we must avoid the flaw that Glenn Tinder finds in Jonathan Schell's widely hailed *The Fate of the Earth*; we must not take our own existence, even as a communal social ecology, as an end in itself.[3]

A deeper question, then, has to be asked about the tie that binds. That second question is the reality question: what is the tie that binds us existentially, forming us into genuine rather than illusory community? When is community real rather than merely apparent? When does a grouping of people in the same time and place, in a shared activity or enterprise, truly unite and thus fulfill them, and when does it merely appear to do so? How do we distinguish between authentic community and its counterfeits? If community is to be a moral norm, telling us what is right and what is wrong in behavior, then community must be real rather than merely apparent, and we must be able to know that it is. What we must do has to be rooted in what we are. Thus a metaphysics, an understanding of what is real not just in human associations but in the rest of the world as well, is essential to any full articulation of the "second language" of *Habits of the Heart*. The tie that binds us morally must first bind us existentially. For if there is no real community, there is

---

[3] See Glenn Tinder's perceptive remarks in "The Secular City." (*The New Republic*, 3, 526 and 527, August 16 and 23, 1982). In reviewing Leszek Kolakowski's *Religion* (London: Oxford University Press, 1982), Tinder sees a basic flaw in the urgent desire of many secular writers for preventing a nuclear holocaust. That flaw is their implicit idolatry in making the survival of our species an end itself. That flaw leads to others, notably an inability to criticize contemporary society in terms of any communal norms. Tinder's *béte noir* here is the widely praised book by Jonathan Schell, *The Fate of the Earth* (New York, Knopf, 1982).

no obligation toward communal practices, toward communal "habits of the heart."

Of the several recent fine theories of community, John Macmurray's *Persons in Relation* most nearly resembles this present attempt to articulate a systematic analysis of community that reaches toward metaphysical roots.[4]   Macmurray and I treat of several of the same principal questions, and use a similar vocabulary. We also reach some of the same conclusions. But *Community: The Tie That Binds* differs in several important respects from Macmurray's books, and from other recent influential writings as well. The primary difference is that this book attempts a purely philosophical analysis of community – one that makes no appeal to religious belief. The method is rigorous in its argumentation; yet the style seeks an interdisciplinary audience. Macmurray and others write from a Christian point of view and for a Christian audience. This approach, then, is distinctive. My hope is for a philosophy of community which, while compatible with Christian and other religious beliefs, makes no appeal to them. Yet, it can aid both believers and those who adhere to no organized religion. At the very least, a philosophical understanding of community clarifies one of the options that we take when we choose to be (or not to be) religious believers.

Macmurray and I share the conviction that persons are innately communal rather than disconnected individuals. Thus the forming of communities is a matter of becoming what we already are rather than contracting for various common goals that are more or less arbitrary. We are also at one basically, though not completely, in locating the unifying core of community in the heterocentric intentions of its members. We both conclude from these two premises that

---

[4] See John Macmurray, *Persons in Relation* (Atlantic Highlands: Humanities Press, 1979), and Frank G. Kirkpatrick's *Community, A Trinity of Models*, which presents a fine overview of Macmurray's book as well as theories of community by Hobbes, Locke, Hegel, Marx, Whitehead, Pols, Buber and others. Kirkpatrick's book, which offers a synthetic, Christian view of community, was published in Washington, D.C., in 1986, by the Georgetown University Press.

I am indebted deeply to Glenn Tinder for his *Community: Reflections on a Tragic Ideal,* published by Louisiana State University Press, Baton Rouge, in 1980.

Another very helpful volume – one of the few philosophical rather than theological or psychological approaches to community – has been edited by Robert Roth, S.J., *Person and Community: A Philosophical Exploration* (New York: Fordham University Press, 1975). Ferdinand Tonniës, *Community and Society* (New York: Harper Brothers, 1957) remains basic, as does Robert A. Nisbet, *Quest for Community* (London: Oxford University Press, 1969).

selective love is anti-communal, that is, that the range of any
community is, at least implicitly and potentially, the entire
human race. We agree that community is a moral norm, an
end or goal that binds us to certain behaviors as being good
simply because they promote community. And we are at one
in seeing community as a very practical reality, a matter not
just of intentions but of appropriate praxis as well.

Given these similarities, as well as the success and influ-
ence of Macmurray's works, a reader might well wonder what
is left for another book on community to do. The basic contribution here is a more clear and extensive analysis of what
Macmurray calls "heterocentric intentions" and what I, for
reasons explained later, choose to call "altruistic love." Making this analysis my premise, I then differ from Macmurray in
several conclusions. I allow for an achievement of total community within present history, not just in the next life. The
achievement of total community is episodic. It is, moreover,
essentially an interior regime which seeks but does not necessarily require any external success. Macmurray apparently
allows only for an imperfect community, one that contains
important anti-communal elements and includes only part of
the human race, as our highest hope this side of the endtime.

I also depart from Macmurray in my view of social and
political structures such as power, law, and justice as well as
the institutions which crystallize these. He allows these as
necessary non-communal elements of community, as negative
elements that are subsumed into the over-arching communal intent of citizens. I argue that law, justice, power, even
war, when properly motivated, are transformed into genuine
communal structures. My dichotomy between community
and contract is more stark, and my view of community more
integral, than Macmurray's. My premises lead to the conclusion that we either have community and have it whole, or we
do not have it at all. Finally, my historical sources are older
than Macmurray's (except for his use of the Bible). I reach
back to medieval and classical Greek sources, primarily the
ethics of Aristotle and the development by Thomas Aquinas
of Aristotelian friendship in the context of a metaphysics of
existential act. The contemporary sources I appeal to, syn-
thesized with Aristotle and Aquinas, are recent continental
thinkers, primarily Gabriel Marcel and Maurice Nédoncelle.

Finally, this book treats of several important topics concerning community that Macmurray and other recent American and British writers treat only briefly or not at all. One of
these grows out of the central paradox that human fulfillment

comes by way of altruistic or heterocentric love. This paradox presents the most formidable challenge to a communitarian view of human relationships: the logic of self-sacrifice. If we are to demand sacrifices by individuals for the sake of community – and no theory of community can avoid making some such demands – we have to ask what the limits of sacrifice are. Our view of the ultimate self-sacrifice, of giving up one's life for the community, is the point of greatest pressure for any coherent philosophical theory of community. By what logic can such sacrifice be understood, admired, and even required (apart from religious considerations of a reward in the after-life)? A second important topic, the problem of evil, is another acid test of the logical coherence of a view that would make altruistic love the tie that binds. What is the place, if any, of men of evil intent in a loving community? I raise the question whether there can be evil communities, or communities of evil-doers, or even evil members of a community that is good overall. My answer to these questions is, in each case, negative. For if altruistic love is the tie, the only tie, that can bind us together existentially, then where love is lacking, so is community. Groupings of people of evil intent are thus mere associations, appearing to be communities but not really so. And evil-doers might exist in spatio-temporal closeness to a given community. But they are, at best, only apparent members of it.

But to hold up altruistic love, the tie that binds, as a norm of morality which enables us to discern which human behaviors are good and which are evil, which communities are real and which are spurious, is not enough. That norm needs to be spelled out in some explicit detail, in a way in which other recent works on community do not attempt. Love needs its guidelines, and for those the present work makes an appeal to the natural law tradition, not so much for specific content of moral precepts but for a method by which we might formulate moral – which is to say, communal – principles of right behavior for our own time.

The book has been some 20 years in the making. Its first stirrings were felt during the civil unrest of the late '60's in the United States, when social organizers such as Saul Alinsky were in their prime. This writer was asked to offer a summer course in the Philosophy of Community as a visiting professor at Marquette University. The effort to prepare such a course soon showed that there was no such field of knowledge, no organized branch of philosophy in which there was an agreed-upon set of problems to be treated, an approved method, a set of coherent conclusions, about community. Some key problems for philosophical reflection occurred almost at once. One was, quite simply, the definition question: what is community? The concept is certainly normative. That is, thinkers in many fields, and of many persuasions, regard community as a value, as a human good. And yet, the definition used in the social sciences did not seem adequate: "a group of people organized for a common purpose, or engaged in a common activity." The Third Reich was certainly such a group and yet not, to put it mildly, a model for the rest of us. And who has not seen families and marriages in which a cloying closeness seems repulsive rather than attractive? Friendships and marriages have slowly died because their members were over-involved in activities with other people and never had time alone together. This writer saw one marriage in particular, in which the wife suffered through ten hellish years with an abusive alcoholic husband. Once he sobered up and stayed that way, the couple enjoyed for another 25 years an exquisite intimacy. Such a marriage seems far preferable to many other more peaceful marriages in which the spouses live separate lives in the same house. What is it, then, that makes people really be one with each other? The question resolves finally into the metaphysical one: when is community real? when is it only apparent? what makes it real? how do we know the difference?

Once we find a satisfactory answer to this reality question, other questions and their answers begin to fall into place, and something like a coherent philosophy of community can gradually emerge. The range of community, its practicality, its relation to religion, to praxis, to law, to social organization, to morality all find explanations that make sense in light of the central premise of altruistic love as the tie that binds. And as this overall view emerges, a point-by-point contrast with social contract theory becomes evident as well. Affinities of this philosophy of community with some of the findings of modern psychologists are striking, particularly with those who see intimacy as the mark of mental health and emotional maturity. Even the work of some sex researchers and sex therapists resonates with this view of community. Finally, questions of social injustice – of world hunger, of racism and sexism, of the arms race and environmental concern – fall into place as community issues. Anyone who holds such a philosophy of community can truly say, with the Roman poet, "Nothing human is alien to me."

My most fruitful sources have been Aristotelian, Thomistic, and Existentialist. The seeds of this proposed philosophy of community, especially in its points of contrast with contractual theories of human associations, are in Aristotle's treatise on friendship in Books VIII and IX of the *Nichomachean Ethics*. The germinal notion of altruistic love there comes to full flower in Aquinas' development of Aristotle's ideas in the context of a creationist metaphysics. Contemporary existentialist thinkers, primarily Gabriel Marcel, provide a phenomenology of human love which suits these earlier theories well, so that metaphysics and concrete daily life meet and embrace.[5] The concluding application of this synthesis of traditional metaphysics and recent phenomenology to contemporary practical concerns of moral, political and social life is my own.

The book could not have happened, though, without the help of many other thinkers and writers, too numerous to name. Written sources are duly acknowledged in footnotes and bibliography. But scholarly apparatus is not adequate to express the writer's dependence on, and gratitude for, the help of many others. When one has been in academic life for more than thirty years, conversations merge and blend, and ideas become one's own in such a way that their origins can no longer be traced. Special thanks thus go to my revered professors and colleagues at Marquette University, both past and present, and to those beloved students who have, over the years, made teaching a two-way street. Most of all, my thanks must go to Edward L. Rousseau, not only for his ideas about community, both spoken and written, but for his steady altruistic love, which is the ongoing source of my being as a philosopher of community.

I am also grateful to Worldwide Marriage Encounter and to the Mellon Foundation for grants that enabled me to write the book. And I am grateful to Marquette University, whose Office of Research Support supplied several grants as well as released time and secretarial help.

---

[5] The main elements of the metaphysics of love that underlies this present philosophy of community are set forth in Robert O. Johann's *The Meaning of Love* (Glen Rock, New Jersey, Paulist Press, 1966). Johann synthesizes a Thomistic creationist metaphysics with the views of such existentialist thinkers as Buber, Marcel, Nédoncelle, Lavelle and Madinier.

CHAPTER I

THE LANGUAGE OF COMMUNITY

Case #1: An old man, falsely accused and convicted of a crime, is sentenced to death. When provided with an opportunity to escape, he declines because of loyalty to the laws as the very source of his being.

Case #2: A young wife and mother of three lives for ten years with an abusive alcoholic husband, despite pleas that both she and her children would be better off without him. Her explanation: "I want to give him a chance to change."

Case #3: A young woman who is an invalid for life, afflicted with cerebral palsy, seeks permission to commit suicide because her life is meaningless. She is fully conscious, of normal intelligence, and able to converse with those around her.

Case #4: A young policeman, husband and father, substitutes himself for a baby who is being held hostage by an armed robber. A few moments later, in the confusion of a shoot-out, he is killed by the bullet of one of his fellow policemen. Later, his city memorializes him as a hero, with a public statue dedicated to the memory of his bravery.

Case #5: An old woman dedicates her life to the care of the simplest needs of people that she finds dying and alone in the streets of a large city. She is honored, with the Nobel Peace Prize, as the person who did more than anyone else in the world to bring about World Peace in the year of our Lord 1980.

All of these cases raise questions about community – about human fulfillment, about the meaning of human life, about how we do and should associate with each other. All illustrate problems with which any adequate philosophy of community must grapple. The first person described above is, of course, Socrates – paradigm of the ambiguities of the relationship of individuals to the state. The second, aunt and godmother to the present author, raises questions about individual fulfillment, about altruism and masochism, about commitment and fidelity, about the more intimate relationships of individuals with each other. The third, Elizabeth Bouvia, is an especially poignant example of one who lives by the implicit values of our present culture, a culture which

1

finds personal worth only in being young, mobile, healthy –
able to "pull one's weight in the boat." These assumptions
all reflect deeper ones, about the nature of human persons,
about relationships and praxis. The fourth person introduced
above is Officer Thomas Buntrock. Some would say that he
was not a hero, but a fool – he gave up his life, and thus
his personal happiness and fulfillment, as well as depriving
his own family of theirs. Better, they would say, to have let
the baby die. Self-sacrifice must always be restrained, balanced by proportionate self-concern. And lastly, a reader will
of course recognize Mother Theresa of Calcutta. Many still
wonder how an individual working with other individuals on
such a small scale, in such an obscure place, and meeting
such minimal physical needs, might have any effect at all on
the wider world. Was her Nobel Peace Prize a mere sentimental gesture, or do the daily actions of ordinary people
have global consequences? Would the world be less peaceful
without Mother Theresa?

The five cases cited above raise most of the main questions which we shall consider in the rest of this investigation
into community. The topic is large and complex, with many
doubts, ambiguities, paradoxes, and controversies. The hope
is that a systematic treatment will resolve the basic controversy in such a way that other doubts and ambiguities will
also be reduced. That basic controversy is between contractual and communal theories of human associations, between
those who make human relationships artificial or conventional and those who make them natural, inborn. Contractual thinkers bring people into unity with each other through
various kinds of agreements, negotiations, conventions, and
arbitrations – labor contracts, for example, or premarital
property agreements, or constitutions. Communal thinkers
take people to be in some kind of unity with each other by
nature, prior to any choices or negotiations. Negotiations
and agreements then merely ratify and specify what is already the case, bringing about various associations between
people that reflect bonds that are already there, bonds that
are right and good because such is the nature of the human
person.

The present investigation is on the communal side of this
long and complicated controversy. Thus, viewpoints on what
constitutes community, on how broad its range may be, on
the role of law and religion, on the utopian objection, and so
forth, will all be spelled out in terms of premises about what
it is to be a human person. Community will be seen as our

way of appropriating a nature that is already ours by birth. But community is not always what it appears to be. There are some severe conditions that we have to meet in order to appropriate our communal nature, and what may look like a community may not be one at all. Conversely, relationships fraught with pain and suffering, seemingly alienating and frustrating to the persons involved, may well turn out to be deeply communal and fulfilling – once the components of genuine community are clearly set forth. Community involves paradoxes within paradoxes, and is achieved in its glorious totality in some unexpected ways. We shall explore, then, a chain of arguments which take up the basic questions about community in an orderly fashion. We begin with some analysis of language.

The first, foundational paradox about community is revealed in the very etymology of the term. *Community* joins two Latin words which, at first glance, contradict each other: the preposition "*com*," meaning "with" or "together," and thus requiring a multitude of at least two; and "*unus*," the number "one" with which we begin to count in Latin. A community, it seems is both one and many – a unified multitude, or a multiple unity of some sort. Community is a "many turned into one without ceasing to be many." Such a concept is a paradox. But it is a necessary one, for a single individual is not a community, nor is just any multitude. A chaotic heap, a disorganized mob is not a community. On the other hand, a solitary individual is alone (literally, "all one"); he is not "with" anyone, not "together." A disordered multitude, in which each one is all one, is not itself unified at all; it is simply many. And yet, the utter absence of multitude, the unity of a single individual, is not a community either.

The ultimate roots of questions about community, then, are metaphysical – the perennial problem of the one and the many. Historically, those roots are in the poem of Parmenides and in Plato's dialogue *Parmenides*. The ultimate question is whether any existent reality can be both one and many, or whether it can be either of those without being the other. The answer of Parmenides in his poem makes community impossible and illusory. For he makes such a sharp dichotomy between unity and multiplicity that never the twain shall meet. Only unity of the purest imaginable kind can be real – the One, which subsumes all that exists. Plato's brilliant critique of Parmenides' dichotomy shows, both logically and dramatically, the disaster which such a view makes of human life. As the dialogue *Parmenides* progresses, it degenerates into utter gibberish. Moreover, that collapse is underlined dramatically when Aristoteles – later to be the tyrant who destroyed communal life in Athens – assents to the gibberish at the end of the dialogue.[6]   Philosophers ever since have tried to describe the unity and multiplicity of things without suppressing either member of the paradox. Some have not succeeded. On the one hand are those who put human associations under the social contract label, who hold that beings, human and otherwise, merely associate in various extrinsic ways, all the while remaining deeply and radically separate from each other. To them, beings are just many and not one at all. Unity is a mere appearance.

Others – the various idealisms – err in the opposite direction, for they make plurality a mere appearance that covers up an underlying complete unity. What appear to be the members of a community, thus diverse units, are ultimately absorbed into a super-one, an individual being whose being is all that there is. The paradox of community is thus a metaphysical challenge, asking us to combine unity and plurality in such a way that both persist and each is, indeed, enhanced by the other.

To put the challenge in terms of human relationships, a philosophy of community must validate the dream of every human heart. That dream is that we might love and be loved, that we might associate with each other, in such a way that closeness and autonomy both survive, and even enhance each other. In our dream, someone – everyone – accepts us, affirms us, praises us, enjoys us just for being who we are. We are recognized as unique and uniquely valuable individuals, encouraged to be ourselves to the utmost, loved in our totality and for our own sakes. And yet, the love that encourages our uniqueness and autonomy brings the warmth and security of total belonging. We and those with whom we live in love are close to each other, intimate, not alone but securely and completely together. In our dream, closeness does not threaten independence but enhances it – and *vice versa*. Those with whom we are most intimate leave us free to be ourselves. We have our cake and eat it too. We belong but are not possessed. We are free but not alone. A three-year-old boy once expressed this common human

6 Parmenides' poem and Plato's dialogue *Parmenides* are well presented by Francis Macdonald Cornford in *Plato and Parmenides: Parmenides' Way of Truth and Plato's Parmenides* (London: Routledge, 1951).

dream, all unawares of the depth with which he spoke. A visitor patted him on the head and asked, "Whose little boy are you?" Our hero drew himself up and replied, indignantly, "I'm nobody's – I am myself!" He was already feeling the pressure of the apostrophe, that tiny linguistic mark of possession. And yet, his little declaration of independence could not have surfaced except for the deeper security of belonging, of being someone's, that he had already experienced. A three-year-old without a home, without ties to a loving family, would have no such base on which to enjoy his independence. He would be nobody's in any sense, possessive or communal, and in thus being nobody's, would be nobody as well.

The dream is shattered, though, by a reality which is, often enough, its double reverse. "Mama," one ten year-old complained, "Amanda thinks that just because I am her friend, she owns me. She thinks that she can tell me who else to play with and who not." Closeness often threatens autonomy. On the other hand, marriages flounder because "our careers just drove us apart." The problem of the one and the many is the stuff of everyday life. Problems of community on a grand scale are not, of course, simple enlargements of those in one-to-one intimacies. But the two are not entirely disconnected. Dag Hammarskjold remarked that while he was Secretary General of the United Nations, and thus concerned with community on a global scale, he always paid careful attention to the various intimacies of his private life. He was sure that without such small intimacies, he could not be an instrument of world unity and peace.[7]   Studies show that crime rates are demonstrably connected to the breakdown of family life, and the nuclear arms race is a direct result of the emergence of nation states. W. H. Auden saw the connection well; he saw the roots of world war in the lives of millions of individuals, each one "seeking not love universal, but to be loved alone."[8] In ancient and medieval times, philosophers supported this

---

[7] See Dag Hammarskjold, *Markings*, translated by Leif Sjoberg and W. H. Auden (New York: Alfred A. Knopf, 1966), pp. 129-130.

[8] See W. H. Auden's poem, "September 1, 1939," in *The Collected Poetry of W. H. Auden* (New York: Random House, 1965). The relevant lines are:

> For the error bred in the bone
> Of each woman and each man
> Craves what it cannot have,
> Not universal love
> But to be loved alone.

dream of the human heart, that closeness and autonomy
might go together, that we might belong without being possessed. There were theories about the human person that
made our various associations natural, right and good. Community was normative for human life. Love was regarded as
a quite realizable ideal, and people found fulfillment rather
than frustration in family life and in political and social organization. Exile was a severe punishment, and those who
shunned human society were scorned as idiotic. But this
communal view no longer prevails among philosophers of the
West, especially in English-speaking circles. Since the Enlightenment, social contract theory prevails and makes of human relationships a series of ongoing negotiations. In our
various contracts, implicit and explicit, large scale and small,
autonomy is repeatedly compromised by closeness, and *vice
versa*. We seek optimal distances from each other. We calculate giving and taking. We balance unity with separation,
vulnerability with safety. We constantly renegotiate, and
when negotiations break down, relationships break up.[9]

This post-Enlightenment, contractarian view of human
associations rests on an assumption about human persons.
We are solitary, detached, atomic units with no natural ties
to each other. The ultimate units of being are individual
egos, each giving primacy to his own striving for fulfillment.
We are centers of freedom and rights – rights that each of us
defines arbitrarily for himself, and freedom to pursue those
rights in doing as we please. We exist, in Hobbes' graphic
phrase, in a "war of all against all." When we do link up
with each other, it is because our free pursuit of our own
rights has come into conflict with someone else's free pursuit
of his own rights. We then have a "conflict of rights," a conflict which could destroy one or both of us. In order to avoid
that destruction, we negotiate a contract. Each of us gives
up some freedom, some autonomy, in order to preserve the
rest. If our association continues and becomes a friendship
or a marriage, a nation or an alliance, we continually renegotiate its terms as our rights continually conflict. We find a
constantly shifting balance between our associations and our
independence, our freedom and our obedience, our closeness
and our autonomy. The "war of all against all" is mitigated,
but it never stops. For the war is inherent to our nature

---

[9] For a concise and reliable overview of social contract theory, see Kirkpatrick,
Community, A Trinity of Models, pp. 13-61.

as solitary, competitive atomic individuals. The unity produced by the social contract is functional but not existential, ephemeral and illusory rather than lasting and real.

The philosophy of community to be presented in these pages harks back to the older, ancient and medieval view that was once a common assumption in both philosophy and everyday life in Western Europe. Our associations with each other, especially when formed with loving intentions, were not then seen as contrivances that were necessary to our survival. Rather than going against the individualistic grain, friendships, polities and other groupings of human beings resulted from free and conscious efforts to be what we already are, to appropriate our inborn communality. The tie that binds did not lock us into power struggles, overt or covert. Obedience to authority and to law was not submission to someone else's control, but the way of bringing our human freedom to its full flower. The skills of interpersonal relationships were not those of shrewd negotiating, but of loving with pure hearts.[10]

Robert Bellah and his colleagues in *Habits of the Heart* find in contemporary American social life and thought a few remnants of the "second language" of community, embedded in the context of a predominant "first language" of individualism. In their view, community was the primary intent of those who founded our country, but that intent failed to survive the industrialization of the nineteenth century. Actually, communal thought and practice had been in its death throes for some time when Jonathan Edwards and others first brought it to our shores. Hobbes and his successors had already brought individualism to the fore among professional philosophers. Hobbes' *Leviathan* appeared in 1651. This seminal work brought about a shift in philosophical thought that was accompanied by a similar shift in the thinking of ordinary people. Webster's Unabridged Dictionary documents startling changes in the usage of a whole cluster of terms referring to community, a shift from communal to individualistic meanings.

Perhaps the most important of such terms, because it refers to the members which must make up any human association, is the term *person*. The term originated among the

---

[10] Medieval views on community were largely developed in the monastic and canon law traditions. See Giles Constable, *Religious Life and Thought, 11th and 12th Centuries* (London, Variorum Reprints, 1979) and Brian Tierney, *Church Law and Constitutional Thought in the Middle Ages* (London, Variorum Reprints, 1979).

Romans, or perhaps their ancestors, the Etruscans, as the name for an actor's mask. Now drama was, and is, a complex event; it is fundamentally communal. Even a soliloquy presupposes an audience. Acting is a process of communicating. Masks are used only by persons interacting with other persons, not when one is at home alone. The actor's mask was meant to reveal to the audience human thoughts and feelings, the human spirit. The audience was made up of persons, too. The point of a mask is lost on family pets and other animals. The origin of the term *person*, then, carries communal connotations. A person is one who communicates with other persons. But as the term has more recently developed in modern English usage, it has taken on a strong individualistic coloring. The first current meaning for person in our dictionary is, "an individual human being," and the original meaning, "a character in a play," is labeled archaic.

The adjective *personal* also has both communal and individualist meanings, and in modern usage the latter has priority. What is personal is now private, "of or relating to the private affairs of an individual." Only in a secondary sense does the word mean, "characteristic of human beings as distinct from things." *Personality* has three references that could be taken as communal: it refers to the complex of characteristics that typify an individual in his relations with others; to the totality of his tendencies in interacting with his environment; or to his distinction in having admirable and influential traits (one is admired by, and influential over, other persons). But these three communal meanings are all secondary to the primary meaning of the term: one's individual identity. In fact, the individualism of current usage is epitomized in Webster's definition of *personal liberty*:

> "the freedom of the individual to do as he pleases, limited only by the authority of politically organized society to regulate his actions to secure the public health, safety or morals."

No other uses are even mentioned. The original communal ideas of liberty, of person, of freedom, authority and morals have been utterly lost to English usage.

A similar loss of communal connotations that once were primary is evident in the changing usage of another set of terms, words that refer to the kind of love once thought to be characteristic of human associations. The terms *kind, generous, humane, free, liberal, gentle,* and *courteous* all enjoyed, in their original usage, primary meanings that made loving, communal behavior normative for human beings. Rather than the freedom to do as we please, subject only to certain legal restraints, a loving generosity was seen as characteristic of our species. This normative reference to love and communality is most evident in the history of the term *kind*. As a noun, *kind* originally meant a species or essence, a type or class, even a family or lineage. It was linked to *kin*, a term derived from Latin, Greek and Sanskrit terms connected with the begetting of children. But the oldest word in that series, the Sanskrit term *jana*, also meant *person*. Thus a person was the epitome of belonging to a loving community. Animals have their ancestors, of course, but they don't have kin. To be a member of a kind and to be a person were originally regarded as one and the same.

The adjective *kind* once had a double meaning that reflects its early references to community as a norm for human beings. But half of that older meaning has become obsolete. The word still means, as it always has, "friendly, obliging, humane." But its earlier meaning also made such attitudes normative. Because of our inborn nature, our belonging to a community through having been begotten by other persons, our kin, what was kind was also "natural, fitting, suitable or right,"– appropriate to our kind. Kindness was the characteristic feature of those born into the human species. Shakespeare's "milk of human kindness" carried both of these meanings. A baby's ability to live in a loving community, to give and receive kindness, was nourished along with his newborn physical life as a member of his kind, the human species. Human kindness was thus rooted in humankindness.

But the normative connotation of kindness has now become obsolete. One dictionary dates its disappearance at around 1700, the time when social contract theory came into philosophical prominence. Parallel changes came about in the usage of terms that are synonymous with *kind*. *Generous*, for example, which now means "loving," once also meant "of noble birth, born into high social status." Love was then taken as characteristic of the high-born. The cluster of terms derived from the Latin *homo*, "human being," reflect a similar shift. Most notable among these is the word *human*, which was originally spelled with a final *e* and carried two meanings. It referred in a normative way to human beings, meaning "characteristic of man in his essential nature." That meaning has been lost, but the other half of its original content persists: *humane* in the sense of "compassionate, sympathetic, considerate." Today we admire humaneness, but as an option. The term no longer connotes that that is what a person ought to be because that is the kind of being he is, that to be human *is* to be humane.

Similar changes in usage are evident in the definitions of *free* and *liberal*. These terms now connote generosity, and the love which generosity bespeaks. But both also referred at one time to those human beings who were normative of human life, who were at the height of human aspirations. A freeman was, in the Sanskrit root of the term, dear, beloved as a member of the family – kinfolk as opposed to a household slave. Such people, not only free politically and socially, loved with a free handed-generosity. In Roman times, a liberal person also enjoyed that double freedom. He was liberated socially and politically, and was free or unrestrained in his generosity as well. In feudal times, the gentle and courteous man played these same two roles, showing a kindness that was normative for members of his kind. A gentleman was, primarily, one born to high station, a model of humanity. But his characteristic behavior was gentle – he was tenderly concerned for his fellows. A courteous person, also gentle and kindly in his behavior, showed himself to be someone who who belonged in a court, along with others of high status in human society. Those who enjoyed high human status were those who loved others – not those who were at war with all.

The prevalence of the idea that community, along with the love which generates it, is somehow natural to us and not a contrivance to restrain our innate hostility is, perhaps, most evident in the etymology of the word *like*. The word originates in a Germanic compound which means, literally, "of the same body," hence "similar to" or "connected with." When the Old English *lician* was current, it meant both "to please" and "to be similar to," a double meaning which surely suggests that we are pleased by what we are similar to, that we like what we are like. It is easy to lay bare the philosophical assumptions behind such language. They are communal rather than contractual. For when we like someone, we see them as like us, as suiting, or matching up with, some feature in ourselves. Love involves a double likening as well as a liking.

The metaphysical roots that distinguish communities from contracts are reflected, then, in the history of our language. For two entities that are entirely alien to each other can never come together as one except in some extrinsic linkage. Solitary individuals, then, no matter how intricate their associations, remain just that. The citizens of Leviathan cannot like each other because they are not like each other. Community can overcome solitude only if solitude is not ultimate. We shall explain this basis for community at length later on. But even the ordinary usage of common terms indicates that community requires, as a basis for our enacting it, a prior communality, a likeness among those who would like each other.

Contractual associations, and theories about them, rest on a different assumption: persons are individuals, and individuals alone. Since their alienation is complete, their solitude total, their only bonds must be extrinsic, links between rivals locked in various conflicts of rights. The conflicts may be negotiated, so that they are then somewhat restrained. Such associations may be quiet, peaceful, enjoyable to everyone involved. But they cannot be gentle or courteous in the root meaning of those terms. Nor can they be fundamentally generous, liberal, or free. Without some prior likeness, there can be no liking. Without humankindness, there can be no human kindness. Atomic physics, as the basic picture of the world, allows only for aggregates of the ultimate particles – never true composite substances. Applied to human relations, atomic physics allows individual persons to associate in time and space – but never to become one in any existential, properly personal way.

This brief excursion into the history of English usage reveals the theme of this book. While the loss of communal connotations to the terms we have just examined may not have been causally linked to the emergence of social contract theory among philosophers, it did coincide with it. And so, it is to a retrieval that we now turn – retrieval not just of older meanings of words like *person, like, kind, human* and *free*, but of the philosophical assumptions on which those meanings were formerly based.

The first sustained and systematic treatise on interpersonal relationships in Western thought is Aristotle's discussion of friendship in books VIII and IX of the *Nichomachean Ethics*. Aristotle is, of course, famous for defining us as political animals. The highest, most perfect life was that of the citizen, actively participating in the life of the *polis*. What is not so well known is that Aristotle also said that we are, more fundamentally, conjugal animals, that marriage is more natural to us than citizenship. He makes family life prior to politics. And in the relationship of husband to wife, the great philosopher sees an instance of the highest possible kind of interpersonal relationship, a friendship of the third kind. In his analysis of friendship, then, we will find certain philosophical principles that must remain at the base of any philosophy of community.[11]

Aristotle's term for *friendship* – *philia* – had a much stronger meaning than our English word. We often say, for example, "No, he doesn't love her – they are just friends." We often hear people say, when asked, for example, if someone who died was close to them, "No, not really – just a friend." Friendship is weak and anemic in our usage, far from the intense closeness and devotion that the Greek *philia* would suggest. In fact, Aristophanes makes it the term for the greatest possible closeness between people. He says that two people who love each other would like to become physically one with each other, to meld into a single person. But since they realize that such a union would destroy one – or both – of them, they do the next best thing. They become friends, living together and sharing life.

In Aristotle's analysis, friends could share life in three different ways, thus generating three different kinds of friendships. The first two – friendships of utility and of pleasure – are similar enough to each other, and different enough from the third, that they can be treated together. They are, in effect, what we would now call utilitarian and hedonistic contracts. In them, men associate with each other because they find each other useful or pleasant. They meet each other's needs, and associate with each other for those reasons. Such friendships are not stable, for people, and thus their needs, change in the course of time. Thus friends of the first two kinds eventually cease to be useful to each other, or cease to enjoy each other. When the basis of their friendship disappears, the friendship comes to an end. People who form such associations can truly be called friends; they are not out to use, abuse, or take advantage of each other. They do meet the minimum requirement for *philia* – reciprocal benevolence or well-wishing. They wish each other well, and have some genuine concern for each other's well-being. Without some

---

[11] Aristotle's discussion on friendship is in books VIII and IX of the *Nichomachean Ethics*. See, for example, Richard McKeon, *The Basic Works of Aristotle* (New York, Random House, 1941), pp. 1058-1093. Two fine recent analyses of this discussion, both by John M. Cooper, are "Aristotle on the Forms of Friendship," (*Review of Metaphysics*, 30, June 1977, pp. 618-648), and "Friendship and the Good in Aristotle," (*The Philosophical Review*, 86, July, 1977, pp. 290-315). Cooper emphasizes that the essential characteristic of *philia*, which generates friendships of the third kind, is wishing well to one's friend for the friend's sake.

Aristotle in fact sees human beings as naturally conjugal, so that marriage is prior to political order. Marriage is seen to be a friendship of the third kind, based on virtue. (VIII, 12, 1162a 16-25).

minimal benevolence, they would be enemies. But they are friends in a secondary, deficient sense of the term.

The primary, perfect kind of friendship is that of the third kind, friendships of virtue. In these more perfect associations, men who are virtuous or morally good associate with each other, and their association itself is a virtue. Such men are true friends, friends in the fullest sense of the term. Their friendships are durable, marked by trust and fidelity. But stability and instability are only superficial marks of difference between virtuous friends and those of the first two kinds. In all these cases, friends wish well to each other. But there are subtle differences in their motives for doing so. The psychology of well-wishing is different in the three cases, and that difference, subtle though it may be, makes a profound difference in the friendships themselves. In friendships of utility and of pleasure, the friends wish well to each other, but each does it for his own sake. The friendship benefits each friend himself, and it is that benefit to himself that motivates, or moves, him to wish well to his friend. The business partner, for example, who has money to invest but no managerial skills might link up with a skilled manager who has no money to invest. The investor wishes well to the manager. He is concerned for his health and welfare. But he is concerned for these for his own sake, not that of his friend. His main goal is the protection of his investment. He looks upon his manager's welfare as a means, not an end. It is something he wishes, and labors for, not because he sees it as good in its own right and wants it to exist for his friend's sake, but because it meets his own needs. He loves himself as an end or purpose, and his friend as a means to that end. He sees his friend's well-being not in absolute terms, but in relation to himself.

Friends who associate because they find pleasure in each other have a similar motive. They wish well to each other, but as a means to an end. Each one wants his friend to thrive, but for his own sake, so that his own pleasure may continue. A woman who links up with another woman who enjoys the same kind of music as herself, for example, befriends the other. They associate with each other, go to concerts together, listen to albums, talk about music. Each wishes the other well, but not for the other's sake. Each wishes her friend to stay well, to thrive, for the sake of her own pleasure, not because she sees the other's well-being as a good in its own right. Each sees the other in relative terms, not as an absolute good. Each loves the other not as an end, but as a means to her own pleasure.

The instability of friendships of these first two kinds is rooted in this self-centered motivation. Our businessman may acquire managerial skills himself, or his partner may lose them. Someone else with even better skills may come along. In any of those cases, the investor will no longer have a motive for associating with his erstwhile friend, and their relationship will dissolve. The instability of friends who base their association on pleasure has the same root. As tastes in music change, the basis of their caring for each other disappears, and so does their friendship. Thus, what marks the deepest difference between friendships of use and of pleasure, on the one hand, and those of virtue, on the other, is not the reciprocal well-wishing which is found in all friendships, but the motivation for such benevolence. Friends of the third kind – real friends – wish each other well for each other's sake. Such men are virtuous, or morally good. They do what is humanly right, what shows the excellence that is distinctive of human beings. Their friendship is itself the supreme instance of such excellence. Their love is normative for human life.

True friends wish each other well, then, but each for the other's sake. Their love is altruistic in its motivation, even as the love of friends for use and for pleasure is egocentric. True friends do not seek their own benefit first and foremost, as their end or goal, and that of their friends as a means to that. True friends see each other's goodness as an end, as a value in its own right, as an absolute good rather than a good that is wholly relative to their own needs. And that altruistic motive makes all the difference in the world. It does not just mark the difference between stable and unstable unions. It makes the difference between real and apparent unions, between associations that are really communal and those that only appear to be so. For altruistic motivation is, for Aristotle and his tradition, the tie – the only tie – that binds. With such love, two people become one with each other while yet remaining two. Without it, two remain two and do not become one at all.

There is a metaphysics behind these distinctions – a theory about the make- up of the human person, and a theory about causality. For Aristotle, a person is, like any other substance found in the material world, such as an animal or a plant, a "*tode ti*," a "this something of a certain kind." Each person is an individual substance or being, not part of any other person, or plant, or animal, not a part or manifestation of a deeper underlying substance, not a mere cluster of atoms temporarily close to each other in space and time. Each person is a substantial being in his own right. And yet, persons all belong to one species, even as do all animals of other kinds, all plants, all minerals. We classify material things into species or kinds because that is the way that they really exist. Each has a form, or a specifying characteristic, which is numerically different from, but specifically the same as, the form found in all other individuals of that kind.

The *tode ti* that is a human person is, then, an individual in his own right, but not an isolated or solitary individual. He has a fundamental link, tie, similarity with all human persons. That link, prior to any of the similarities and compatibilities which lead us to link up with each other in various kinds of associations, is our common humanity. Prior to any freely chosen generosity in our associations with each other is an ontological generosity. That ontological generosity is the form of our very being, the specifically human form in each of us linked, by similarity, to the specifically human form in everyone else.[12]   In the later, happy phrase of Boethius, a person is "an individual of rational nature." The nature that we share is a natural communality into which we are born. We come to life as members of a kind, with ontological, existential links to our kin. The rationality that constitutes human nature as distinct from all other natures is the capacity for altruistic love, for friendships of the third kind. For rationality is our ability to recognize our kind, other individuals of a rational nature, and take a basic stance toward them. In that basic stance, we can overlook our kinship and thus refuse our kindness. In that case, we do not form friendships of any type. Our natural communality does not become community. We can, on the other hand, recognize, and associate with, our kin, thus forming friendships. And we can form such friendships in two ways, depending on our motivation. We can associate with our kin for our own sake, in egocentric friendships of use and of pleasure. Or we can do what individuals of a rational nature ought to do, what is right and suitable, what achieves our properly human excellence: we can associate with each other for altruistic motives, thus forming true friendships in which we elevate our natural

---

[12] See the seminal article by Kenneth L. Schmitz, "Community, Elusive Unity," (*Review of Metaphysics*, 37, 1983, pp. 243-64).

I have emphasized the need for social and political structures to be informed by altruistic love in "Community, Elusive Unity, Indeed," (*The New Scholasticism*, 60, 3, Summer 1986, pp. 356-365).

communality to the state of true community.

But how does altruistic motivation tie people together? How does altruistic love unite people where egocentric love does not? Here, we must appeal to Aristotle's understanding of causality, that mysterious process in which one individual being acts upon another and changes it. For the key to altruistic love is the process of identification. Essentially, in order to love someone altruistically, I must identify that person as my other self. Among the Sufi mystics, a proverb would one day emerge: "A man hasn't truly loved until he looks at another and says, 'Hello, myself!'" To identify means "to make the same as." In Aristotle's foundational analysis of community in friendships of the third kind, a true friend sees the other as his other self. He makes the other's welfare his own, loving his friend in his very identity as a person, wishing him, for his sake, to flourish fully as the person that he is. Such identification brings about an ontological union between the two people, through the first friend's causality. For Aristotle, the activity of a cause originates from the cause, but takes place in the effect. Thus, when a friend wishes for another's welfare, and labors to bring it about, that welfare of the other becomes his own as well. As the effect of his causal activity, it is an extension of his own being. The good that he effects in his friend is, in reality, his very self in action.

Aristotle cites a simple but telling example: the loving mother, who seeks her child's welfare for the child's sake, expecting no return for herself. She seeks no gratitude or praise, no reciprocal gift; her child may never even know of her many labors on its behalf. And yet the mother seeks that child's fully flourishing well-being as a person, even if that well-being means a separation from her. She wills that separation as the child's good, for the child's sake. The mother in the film *Kramer vs. Kramer* is a good contemporary example. Even though she had won a hard battle to gain legal custody of her son, she left the boy with his father because she saw that the boy's life there was good for him. On Aristotle's terms, she came to be more one with her son in separating from him, for his sake, than she would have done in taking him with her, for her own sake. For when anyone, in loving altruistically, chooses to identify another's good as his own, that good does become the lover's own. The mother, in the very act of wishing for her son's welfare for his sake, made that welfare her own, no matter how far she might be separated from him in space and time. She came into true friendship, true community, with him by extending her own being (as cause) into his (as effect). In Aristotle's words, "benefactors love their handiwork as their very selves in action, as their own being."

This view of altruistic love is the theme of the theory of community to be elaborated in the rest of this book. It is the norm for discerning between genuine and apparent community. Where there is altruistic love, there is community, and where there is not, there is not. Such love is, ideally, reciprocal, but not necessarily so. When even one person loves altruistically, community becomes real, and all the implications of real community follow. In Aristotle's words, "friendship consists in loving rather than in being loved."[13]

Often these occur together as friends love each other, for each other's sake. But when they do, each lover is more a friend than the one loved, each is a friend because he loves. When we wonder, then, whether we have friends, and who they are, and how many, we must ask not whether others love us, but whether we love, and whom, and how well. And this primacy of loving over being loved remains even in those blessed friendships in which love is reciprocal, in which both friends love and both are loved. The active loving, not the passive receiving of love, constitutes the tie that binds. In all matters of community, without any exceptions, it is truly more blessed to give than to receive. Indeed, giving is the only way in which we can receive.

Aristotle's metaphysics of the person as a *tode ti*, and his view of an effect as an extension of its cause's being, also underlie the deficiencies of utilitarian and hedonistic contracts, those friendships of use and of pleasure that are motivated by egocentric love. One who loves a friend, who wishes his friend well and associates with him, for the sake of his own benefit, seeks rather to be loved than to love. His desire is for his own fulfillment inasmuch as others can give him the various goods that he needs. Such friends love themselves first and foremost. Their love does, indeed, depart from themselves, and extends to others, in a concern for the well-being of those others. But the departure of their love from its center in themselves is only momentary, a step in a circular journey

---

[13] The basis of the unity of friends of the third kind is, for Aristotle, the causal link between the lover's action and the beloved's well-being. For Aristotle, causal action is from the agent (thus being his activity), but in the receiver (thus binding the two together). So the effect of a lover's activity is an extension of the lover's being, his very self in action, residing in his beloved, sharing the beloved's being. See *Nichomachean Ethics IX*, 7, 1168a 2-8.

which ends where it began, within the original self. Such
love constitutes no bond, no union, between lover and loved.
An investor who loves his manager in this fashion forms no
community with him, but only appears to do so. For his own
private good, his profit, is what he sees and cares about primarily. And so, that is all that he possesses. His causality
steps out toward the welfare of his manager, but ultimately
circles back into himself. And so, there is no extension of his
being, even though, as friend and not enemy, he does will his
manager's welfare. The two share no common good. They
are only a pair of private individuals, adjacent in space and
time.

By now, a reader will have noticed a fairly severe problem of language in this proposed philosophy of community.
To use the term *love*, and *altruistic love* in particular, to refer to the basic and recurrent theme of our discussion is to
invite a confusion that is also basic and recurrent. The confusion is due to the same linguistic shift that we noted earlier.
For the terms *love, altruism, egoism* and their cognates show
the same history as do such terms as *person, like, human,*
and *kind.* Whether by coincidence or not, these terms have
lost an earlier, communal meaning in favor of current usage
that assigns them meanings which are primarily contractual.
In our general culture, hardly any other word has more ambiguities than *love*, whose chief connotation is probably the
cheap sexual liaisons portrayed in our popular entertainment.
In more philosophical circles, altruism is immediately associated with the modern controversy which opposes altruism to
egoism and seeks to establish one or the other of these as the
basic human drive. The bewildering swirl of meanings and
connotations around references to love, especially to altruistic love, almost make the phrase unusable in a discussion that
seeks to be clear and precise. And yet, no other term besides
altruism carries the intended meaning. The book, then, uses
this terminology, trusting that its meaning and implications
will become clear as the discussion progresses.

One important and basic confusion grows out of the modern opposition of altruism to egoism, which makes love of
another and love of self opposites. In this modern debate,
egoism is, as its etymology suggests, love of one's self, self-
seeking, a desire for one's own fulfillment. Pure egoism is
abhorred as brute selfishness and as destructive of friendship
and other associations between people. But pure altruism is
also scorned, as a masochism or self- sacrifice which foolishly
destroys its own agent. Concern for the well-being of another

is seen as denial of one's own. The ongoing problem in the controversy is to find ways of balancing the two – to negotiate contracts in which rampant egoism is tempered by just the right degree of altruism, and masochistic altruism is healed by an injection of just the right degree of egoism. "Do something for yourself, for a change," we tell the harried mother or devoted wife. "Can't you think of anyone but yourself? Try putting your family first once in a while," we might say to a selfish adolescent. The key to contractual relations is to resolve these two opposite tendencies into some sort of a manageable synthesis.[14]

But in Aristotle's view, altruism and self-love are not opposites. Rather, they coincide. The man who, in seeking not so much to be loved as to love, devotes himself to a friend's well-being for that friend's sake, thereby becomes his own best friend in the process. One of the recurrent paradoxes about the love that generates community is that it is the highest form of self-love, not a diametric opposite. The reasoning that leads to such a conclusion is not difficult: to love is to wish a good to someone. Thus, to love oneself is to wish what is good for oneself. But what is good for oneself is the extension of one's being into the life of a beloved, forming community with him through the common possession of a single good. My friend's good is my good, too – in and through my identifying it as my own. Our communion in the possession of a single good comes about, paradoxically, in only one way: by my wishing that beloved friend's good to him, for his sake. Such wishing is altruistic, centered on my other self. But that other self is truly mine – and so is his well-being. Paradoxically, then, self-love is a desire for one's own fulfillment, but the fulfillment comes only in loving another for that other's sake. Self-love and altruism coincide. Or, as Aristotle puts it, one who loves another in a friendship of the third kind is, by that very fact, his own best friend. Self-fulfillment comes in and through self-gift.

The paradox has its reverse side as well. Contrary to modern assumptions, an egocentric lover is not on the path to his own fulfillment, not loving himself too much, but quite the reverse. The reasoning is similar: to love is to will a good to someone, and to love oneself is to will a good to oneself. But

---

[14] For a clear and concise summary of the egoism-altruism debate in modern philosophy, see Robert B. Ashmore, Jr., "Ewing on 'Higher' Egoism," (*The New Scholasticism*, LI, 4, Autumn 1977), pp. 513-523.

an egocentric love, in which one wishes the good of another
for his own sake, not for the sake of the other, brings no added
good to the self. An egocentric friendship does not extend
the lover's being into the life of another, and does not bring
about a communion in which two possess a single good in
common. The egocentric friend remains isolated in his own
being, and thus not fulfilled by an increase of the good he
possesses. Paradoxically, the self-fulfillment that he desires
is frustrated because he makes it his motive. Self-seeking
thus leads to self-destruction rather than to self-fulfillment.
Egoism and self-love do not coincide, but are opposed. As a
slogan once had it, "A man all wrapped up in himself makes
a mighty small package."

In falsely opposing altruism and self-love, modern usage
also tends to equate altruism with masochism. Self-sacrifice
is seen as giving up one's own well-being for the sake of others. Such masochism is, at least, unhealthy, and, at the extreme, foolish rather than heroic. The height of self-sacrifice
is in giving up one's life for another, or for a community,
and where's the fulfillment in that? How can one find meaning and fulfillment in an act which terminates his very existence? But Aristotle's altruistic love, the love that is motivated by the welfare of a friend for the friend's sake, differs
from masochism in at least three important ways. First, it
does, automatically and as a matter of undeniable fact, bring
about fulfillment for the one who loves. *Philia*, friendship of
the third kind, is not a form of self-denial, not a way of giving up one's own welfare for the sake of another. Altruism
automatically increases the being, extends the human existence, of the one who exercises it. To take a simple example,
the mother who sacrifices her sleep in order to care for her
sick child does not suffer a net loss. She loses sleep, yes, but
she gains a greater good. For her child's health becomes her
good also, and she thus exists in his life as well as in her own.

Altruistic love also differs from masochism in that it does
not require any diminution or destruction of one's self. Indeed, the logic of love is quite the reverse. One who would
love another altruistically, wishing his good to him for his
sake, puts himself at the service of that good. There is no
sense in saying, "Well, I want good things for you, but don't
expect me to do anything to bring them about." A lover
puts his time and energy, his material and psychological resources at the service of his beloved. Most deeply, he puts
his very self at his friend's disposal. It follows that such a
lover must have time and energy, must have both material

and psychological resources, must have a self to put at his friend's disposal. Self-development, then, is not opposed to altruism, but is one of its prerequisites. If we would love, we must establish our identities, nourish our self-esteem, develop our talents – all for the sake of those we love. A mother who takes time away from her family to pursue her own interests, to develop her talents, or to find joy in relaxed solitude is not detracting from her love for them, but is, rather, enhancing it – provided, of course, that her motive is altruistic.

Altruism and masochism differ on a third important score: a masochist seeks no return from those he serves. He wants no gratitude or praise, no return favors, no reciprocal love. Love is one-sided. As soon as love is returned or rewarded, the sacrifice loses its value. But one who loves as a friend of Aristotle's third kind welcomes every iota of mutuality. The paradigm of altruistic love is not the mother sitting up all night with a sick child. Such one-sided, self-sacrificing love is good as far as it goes and is, as we have seen, as fulfilling for the mother who gives it as for the baby who receives it. But the epitome of *philia* for Aristotle is a reciprocal love between adults who are equals, a friendship in which both love altruistically, each taking the other as his other self, each identifying the other's welfare as his own. Surprisingly, the example the Greek philosopher gives is the marital bond, in which husband and wife become friends of the third kind. In an ideal marriage, each gives the other his total devotion, and each welcomes and receives that total gift from the other.

The logic of such mutuality is not hard to follow. Once again, to love is to wish a good to someone, and offering love altruistically is the highest fulfillment that a human being can find. It follows, then, that if I love someone as a friend of the third kind, there are two very precious offerings I will make to him. I will wish my friend to have the great privilege of loving altruistically, too, and will offer him the opportunity to do so. I will, in psychological jargon, give him permission to love me. I will teach him how to love me, if that is necessary. I will accept his efforts, encourage them, believe and rejoice in the love that he offers to me. For in so doing, I will make my friend's human fulfillment possible. But further, the reciprocity of our love will generate the second good that I must wish for anyone with whom I would have communion: a double joy, rapture, ecstasy.

In a word, when we love, we will play. Play is what we do when all the work is done, when all needs have been

met, at least for the time being. But the height of love, of
friendship and of community is not found in the labors of love,
in which we serve each other's needs. Such laboring service is
certainly an important part of any altruistic love. It would be
a poor love, indeed, not a love at all, that never did any of the
work. But it is an equally poor love that never does anything
else but the work. The high point of love, of altruism and
friendship, is play. And play is joy. Play is rapture. Play is
ecstasy. Play is the simple contemplation and enjoyment of
the good that we see already existing in each other. Thus,
the altruism that seeks the joy of mutual ecstasy, of love-play,
as its high point is a far cry from masochism. Altruism is the
paradox in which we seek our fulfillment in communion with
others, in the joy of reciprocal loveplay. And yet, we are not
motivated by that fulfillment. For it comes only as a side-
effect of a self-sacrificing devotion to the fulfillment of those
we love, a devotion which is for their sakes rather than our
own. But such devotion – realistic, mutual, playful – is a far
cry from masochism.

Altruism in the communal tradition, the tradition which
antedates the social contract views that have influenced English usage for the past three centuries, is thus not opposed
to egoism taken simply as love of one's self. In the modern
egoism-altruism controversy, egoism is equated with conceit,
with selfishness, with the desire to find one's own fulfillment
at the expense of other people's fulfillment. In ordinary usage, self-love is equated with selfishness. Egoists, then, use
their money, time, energy and other resources for their own
sakes, with minimal regard for the well-being of others. And
even that regard is selfishly motivated. The pathological extreme is, of course, sadism. And we show our contempt even
for its milder forms in such sayings as "You can always count
on him to look out for #1," and "Don't you ever think of
anyone but yourself?" Self-love is narcissistic even as altruism is masochistic. And egoism and altruism are in constant
conflict with each other.

Since the time of Hobbes, social thinkers as well as ordinary folk have been wary of all human associations, from
friendships to international relations, because of the strength
of our innate egoism. Contract theory sees all problems of
human relationships in terms of this opposition between altruism and self-love. Solitary individuals, acting out of self-
interest, come into conflicts with other solitary individuals
seeking their self-interests. And then, we must temper our
egoism with just the right touch of altruism, or we will all

perish, at each other's hands. We all mitigate our egoism by making carefully calculated concessions to the egoism of others. Such concessions are then labeled altruistic because they consist in wishing well to others, even though their motives remain egocentric. A contractual self wishes well to others for his own sake, to avoid being a causality in the "war of all against all."

Egoism, then, in the usual modern sense, with its connotations of self-seeking and selfishness, is the very reverse of self-love. But in terms of the Aristotelian paradox, an egoist does not love himself too much, but too little. He is not his own best friend. Indeed, he is not a friend to himself at all. For in seeking his own fulfillment as the motive for his links with other people, his will takes a self-defeating turn. In centering his love – even his benevolence toward others – on the final goal of meeting his own needs, he makes his self-fulfillment impossible. Such men, friends of the first two kinds, certainly gain benefits for themselves from the utilitarian and hedonistic contracts that they enter into and depart from. Their friends are, after all, useful to them and enjoyable. But these rewards are won at the price of a higher good, namely, the extension of their being into the life of their friends, by acting as causes who identify the good of the other as their own. Hobbes' example is striking: he gave money to a beggar one day, and when his companion praised him for his generosity and benevolence, Hobbes explained that he did it for himself. He was distressed at the sight of the beggar's distress, and so acted to give relief to another in order to relieve his own distressed feelings. In the jargon of modern psychology, he did it in order to feel good about himself.[15]

A genuinely altruistic lover, in the classical sense of the term, would, of course, give the money, and feel good about himself afterwards as well. But the difference in motivation, subtle though it may be in its dynamics, is all-important as far as the ontology of community is concerned. An altruist, a friend of the third kind, would be motivated by a desire to help the beggar for the beggar's sake, taking the beggar's good as his own. And that good would then be his own. Motives are psychological events, but they produce real effects.

---

[15] Aubrey reports this telling episode in the life of Thomas Hobbes: an alms that he gave to a beggar in *order to* relieve his own distress at the sight of the beggar's distress – altruism with an egocentric motive. See *John Aubrey's Brief Lives*, ed. Oliver Lawson Dick (London: Secker and Warburg, 1949), p. 157.

An altruistic lover moves his will out of himself and extends it into the one he loves. If we may believe Hobbes' account of his gift, no such extension of his being, no such communion with the good of another, could take place. For Hobbes was motivated by his own self-interest. The good on which his will was fixed was his own good feelings. He did not, then, identify the beggar's good as his own. He extended his loving concern outward to the beggar, thereby extending his own being and coming into communion with another, for a moment – but only for a moment. In the final moment, his love reached out to the beggar's good only as a step toward circling back to Hobbes' own good, his own good feelings. He was a solitary individual when the transaction began, and, even though he felt better afterwards, he was as solitary then as before.

An egoist, then, in the ordinary use of the term, is not a lover of himself, not his own best friend. For he precludes his own enjoyment of community. He, indeed, is the true masochist, giving up his deepest, existential fulfillment. Self-seeking is, paradoxically, self-defeating. It is not a form of self-love that needs to be mitigated by a certain amount of altruism in order to stay healthy. It is utter and complete destruction of the self. In the tradition which this book seeks to retrieve, an egoist, or lover of self, doesn't dilute his self-seeking by certain carefully measured doses of concern for the well-being of others, for his self-love is altruistic. He does not seek to balance opposites by limiting them to calculated portions. For any self-seeking that is true to itself becomes totally converted to benevolence.[16]

The benevolence of a true friend is constant and without limit, a total readiness to give up his life for his friend. Any lapse in such benevolence, any change of his motivation away from his beloved's well-being and toward his own, does not merely reduce his altruism. It utterly destroys it. In this older tradition, the love of self that is identical with love of others is totally and constantly fulfilling to those who enact it. As egoism and altruism coincide, so do self-sacrifice and self-fulfillment. The lover who is the basic unit of true community thus loves himself without limit, even as he loves others without limit.

Such love is both altruistic and egoistic, but not in the

---

[16] In Nédoncelle's striking and utterly precise terms, ". . . an eros that is sincere ...discovers that its vocation is to convert itself to liberality." See Johann, *The Meaning of Love*, p. 78.

current sense of either of these terms. Hence our use of the term *altruism* to refer to the reality that is at the base of any kind of genuine community is quite problematic, given the post-Enlightenment connotations of these terms. And yet, the linguistic problems with other terms seem even more severe. There is no English term, either technical or ordinary, that carries this precise Aristotelian meaning. We could, for example, call such love *benevolent, generous, kind, sensitive, tender, friendly*. Altriusm is all of these and more. But these attitudes can have egocentric motivations – as did Hobbes in his gift to the beggar. And then they are no longer the kind of altruism that generates community. Kindness, liberality, freedom and liking others are no longer what they once were, either. The problem is not just one of language. We lack a vocabulary because we lack the understanding of community. The reality that we wish to discuss hasn't been discussed, and so, its vocabulary is not available.

We shall continue, then, to use the term *altruistic love* and to risk its being confused with masochism and contractual limits on egoism, even though these connotations are later accretions which distort its meaning. I can only ask of my readers an effort to match my own to clarify the usage of the term as the argument progresses. For the love that builds community, the tie that binds, is self-fulfilling; it is unifying, it is generous, benevolent, and kind. It is also beautifying, active, courageous, self-sacrificing, and rare. In varying contexts, any of these features can be paramount. But basic to them all is altruism – the heterocentric motivation by which one loves his friend for his friend's sake rather than his own. That altruism is what makes such love unifying, and is thus the basic concern in an investigation into what makes community real. The fact that such love is not opposed to love of self, but rather coincides with it, is one of which we shall have to frequently remind ourselves.

The antonym of altruism, then, is not egoism, but social contract, especially as various contractual views of human relationships grow out of certain assumptions about the make-up of human persons and of the rest of reality. In contractual theories, predominant since Hobbes, the basic unit of any grouping of people is the solitary ego with no pre-social links to other solitary egos. Links have to be constructed, and all such links threaten and reduce the autonomy of the individual. Aristotle has shown such associations to be, of their very nature, egocentric in their motivation. They are friendships of use and of pleasure. I shall argue that such intrinsically egocentric motivation necessarily precludes community. Contractual associations are of their very nature anti-communal. Contractual associations constitute, not genuine community, but counterfeits of community which more or less successfully, and more or less permanently, conceal a radical plurality that is ultimately hostile and not really unified.

The altruism that is the alternative to social contracts takes, as the ultimate unit or member of community, the individual person who, though unique in all the world and existentially autonomous in regard to other such individuals, is also a member of a natural community that is prior to any socialization. In this context, associations are not mere efforts to mitigate and cover up a war of all against all. Instead, when we form links with each other in friendships and other associations, we freely and consciously appropriate in our personal lives what is already the case existentially. We are born into a natural communality which enables us to identify each other as each other's other selves. Because of this natural communality, the love which generates community is normative for human behavior. It is the way in which we ought to act because it is the way in which we already exist. Altruistic love is the ultimate moral norm, the tie that binds us morally even as it binds us existentially.

A simple example can illustrate such moral implications. In contractarian thought, there might be nothing wrong, legally or morally, with a man's solitary drinking bout behind closed doors. What each person does on his own time, with his own money, to his own body, is his business and no one's else's. The slogan of those feminists who seek to justify abortion on demand – "A woman has the right to do what she wants with her own body"– epitomizes this individualistic view. But on communal assumptions, what a man does behind closed doors on a Saturday night is a concern for the whole community, and not his private business. For even if our drinker does no violence to anyone else, even if he spends money that is his to spend, and does not deprive his wife or children of support, he harms them as well as the rest of the community that he lives in. Even though he sobers up and gets to work on time on Monday morning, the mere fact that during the drinking bout he deprived the rest of us of his inner being, of his clear thoughts, his loving intentions, and his presence makes his behavior morally wrong. He has violated his own communal nature by withdrawing from the love which makes community real.

In the words of a plaque that the author found at an Arts and Crafts Fair in 1982, in Polson, Montana:

> Be what you is,
> because
> If you be what you ain't,
> then
> You ain't what you is.

CHAPTER II

THE TIE THAT BINDS

Socrates, Aunt Catherine, Elizabeth Bouvia, Officer Buntrock, Mother Theresa – all of these cases at the beginning of Chapter I raise questions about the place of community in human life. Was Socrates' apology to Crito logically coherent? Can the state both give life and take it away? And spouses who remain faithful through difficult times – are they hopelessly masochistic? Does an invalid's life have meaning? Do those who voluntarily give up their lives in defense of the innocent find some human fulfillment in so doing, or is their sacrifice a total renunciation? Is Mother Theresa a fool, an admirable fool, perhaps, but a fool nevertheless? All of these questions, and others as well, find answers in social contract theory, and in a philosophy of community. But the answers will differ in the two philosophies, because these two views of human relationships and associations differ in their presuppositions about the meaning of human life. They differ as well in their deeper assumptions about what the members of any community are, about the make-up of human persons and of the world in which we live. They differ most profoundly in their pre-suppositions about what is real and what isn't, what is genuine and what is illusory, and about the ways in which we know the difference.

The core of the present philosophy of community lies in Aristotle's view, which we have just examined, of altruistic motivation as the unifying bond between friends of the third, most perfect kind. That altruism is the basic premise for the argument throughout the rest of this inquiry. It is the basis for all our conclusions about the range and the practicality of community, about its moral force and content, its relation to law and political order, its tolerance of evil. But the notion needs a fuller development than what we find in Aristotle. For one thing, Aristotle's *tode ti*, his doctrine that persons (and other beings of nature as well) are both individuals and instances of various kinds or classes, needs to be rooted in a broader understanding of the larger world. For the process of identification, the crucial element in the altruism by which a lover takes his beloved to be his other self, has to have an objective ground. If there is no reality in another person which justifies my identification with him, then my identification is illusory, a bit of wishful thinking. And with such an illusion, altruism becomes illusory, too, and then so does community.

Without the love of another self for that other's sake, I am
not really tied to, or unified with, my friend. We are only
linked externally, in time and space, in common projects, in
shared ideas. But we remain, in the final analysis, two individuals, as solitary as before. We shall see, however, that
a common humanity is not a sufficient ground for altruistic
love.

The flaw in Aristotle's brief and somewhat cryptic analysis of friendship, especially as that is rooted in his idea of
a person as "a this something of a certain kind," is the dan-
ger of an emphasis on the "certain kind" to the detriment of
the "this something." That is, individuality is easily lost in
Aristotle's theory of specific forms. Individuals can be taken
as interchangeable, as mere instances of a nature or essence,
all alike, and thus all to be treated alike. Thus, while all who
belong to the human species are alike in having that specific
form, it is difficult to explain how individual differences can
be taken into account. A common humanity is a fine basis
for civic equality, for granting the same human dignity and
human rights to all members of the human species. It can be
the basis for a certain sympathy by which we wish certain elements of human well-being to all of mankind. In fact, given
his times, Aristotle goes quite far in that direction, especially
in his scattered remarks about the equality of spouses in a
marriage. But his emphasis on our common humanity is not
matched by an equal emphasis on our individuality, on the
precious differences among people that any community needs
to cherish and nurture.

If we had nothing more to go on than Aristotle's rudimentary analysis, we might have the core of a solid philosophy of
community, but it would easily be perverted into a false uni-
versalism. We would then not discriminate in the bad sense,
treating people differently on the basis of sex, color or age,
when these features are not the point. And so, we would offer
equal rights to both blacks and whites, both men and women,
both old and young. But with such a universal sympathy, we
would lose a more important and valuable kind of discrimi-
nation, the kind we mean when we speak of someone having
a discriminating taste in wines, for example. We would not
be able to recognize differences, and to treat different people
differently, when it was appropriate to do so. In other words,
if a common human nature is the only basis for one person's
identification of another as his other self, then the friendship
becomes abstract instead of real. As Charlie Brown put it,
"I love mankind. It's people I can't stand." And that way

lie all the evils of mass man, of bureaucracy and, ultimately, totalitarianism. Oddly, treating people equally as human beings can lead to reducing them to interchangeable ciphers. Such an abstract community is illusory, not real. It joins a lover to an abstract humanity, thus to a concept in his own mind, and not to the concrete individuated person who is his really existent other self.

A consequence of this view is the absence of a ground on which we could justify self-sacrifice. The justification of self-sacrifice is the ultimate pressure-point for distinguishing a genuine community from an association that is really contractual and just appears to be a community. Indeed, if the other is my exact counterpart in a common humanity, why should I prefer his welfare to my own? How can it make sense for me to give up my life for another? Lesser sacrifices may make some sense. I find a paradoxical fulfillment for myself in giving some of my time, say, or my energy, in order to help a friend. His welfare becomes mine through my identification with it, and so, in communion with his good, I find my own self extended and increased. There is fulfillment for me in that – provided the price is not too high. So long as the good I lose is outweighed by the good I gain, my self-renunciation is rational. But it is all too easy – inevitable, in fact – to lapse into egocentric motives during such *quid pro quo* calculations. The relationship then becomes contractual rather than communal. Contractual views of human relationships can allow for self-sacrifice that is less than the ultimate one, the giving up of my life. It is often to my benefit – for my use, for my enjoyment – to put myself out in order to do something beneficial for another person. If I pay him a good wage, he will give me a good service. If I am pleasant to her, she may be pleasant to me. The *quid pro quo* of a contract makes the *quid* worth the *quo*.

But why should I give up my life? In contractual thinking, such a sacrifice is the height of foolishness. When what I give up is life itself, I get no return, no compensation at all. Such a contract is foolish, for it allows only one winner, the other, and that winner takes all. The difficulty, the logical puzzle about self-sacrifice, is just as acute, though, in a communal context. For the paradoxical fulfillment resultant to altruism seems not to happen, either. How do I find myself fulfilled by communion with the good of another when the price of that good is my very life? How did Officer Buntrock find fulfillment for himself when he became a hostage so that a little girl might live, and then lost his life a few short min-

utes later? Clearly, the altruism which is the tie that binds
needs a more extensive analysis. (Of course, religious belief
in a next life, where such sacrifice receives an eternal reward,
solves the puzzle. But we are prescinding from such beliefs.)

That more extensive analysis can be found in the metaphysics of love developed by Thomas Aquinas, especially as
it is further interpreted in the light of the personalism of
Gabriel Marcel, Louis Lavelle, Maurice Nédoncelle and other
contemporary French philosophers. The basic premise, our
starting point, is empirical. That is, the metaphysics of human love rests on a few simple and ordinary facts of the daily
experience of ordinary people. Those facts show human persons to be both finite and self-transcendent, simultaneously
limited in several fundamental ways and yet able to heal those
limitations. We experience ourselves as limited in being human, for example. True, to be and to be human is a positive
actuality, certainly better than not being at all, and better
than being some lower kind of entity. But there are limitations in being human, too. For to have that specific kind of
existence is automatically not to have others. That lack of
existence shows up most clearly in our inability to do certain things – to fly like a bird, to breathe water as fish do, to
nourish ourselves on inorganic minerals as do the plants. But
the restrictions on what we can do are rooted in restrictions
on how we exist, on how our being is limited by our specific
form. "Please," we say, when asked to do something that is
beyond our innate powers, "I am only human." That "only"
marks the specific finitude of our being.

But being only human has its further restrictions, too,
for no one of us has the fullness even of human existence. We
are sexed beings, for example, each of us enjoying the human
existence of either male or female humanity, but lacking the
other. Further, each of us is an individual, a single member
of a multitude of human beings, one out of many. Of course
we treasure our individual uniqueness, and that of other persons as well. But it is a limitation. To be only this individual
and no other is an ontological loneliness, a lack of the human
existence that we would otherwise have if we were not individuals. In one episode of the TV series "United States,"
the wife was straining against this loneliness, prying into her
husband's psyche, trying to force him to verbalize his feelings. He called her attention to our individual finitude when
he finally exclaimed, in desperation, "Please, Libby, only one
of us can be me."

Being only human and being only this individual human do not tell the whole story, however. We also experience, day in and day out, the finitude of existing in time and space. Our limits in time were noticed and described eloquently by St. Augustine, and thinkers ever since who have pondered that fact have wondered whether we can ever truthfully say that we exist at all. We seem to be constantly passing out of, and coming into, existence, but never to arrive there and stay. To exist in time means, first of all, to have a beginning and an end. Each of us occupies, through our entire life-span, only a very tiny part of all the time that has been and that may yet come to be. Seventy-five years? Ninety-five, even? What is that in comparison to the two hundred years of the existence of our country, to all of human history, to the entire life- span of mankind since its origins? And what are those paltry two or three million years, when measured against the age of the earth, of the solar system, of the universe itself?

But temporal limits, a beginning and an end to each of our lives, do not constitute our deepest limitation in time. More important is the fact of succession in our existence, what one writer has called our "tragic dispersal in time." As our ordinary daily experience shows, we do not enjoy even our limited span of time all at once, but in a succession of moments, each of which must be lost before the next can be gained. There are certainly advantages to being mature, but there is also a deep loss in no longer being a child, or an adolescent – "If only I knew then what I know now ..." "If I could live my life all over again, I'd ..." And the loss is more acute than we usually realize. Just as we no longer have the portion of our limited existence that we had five, ten, twenty years ago, or five, ten, twenty minutes ago, we no longer have even the existence that we had at the beginning of the sentence which is ending here. Nor do we have, at the beginning of this next sentence, the part that we shall have at its end – which we have now, but only at the price of losing what we had at its beginning. Human existence is a constant temporal flow, as well as being enclosed between a beginning moment of each one's life and its end.

Spatial limits, too, are part of the frustrations and the finitude that we experience. We occupy, each of us, only a tiny part of all the space that there is. True, we can move around, travel, come to occupy spaces that are new to us – one advantage of being persons instead of rocks or stationary plants. But each move exacts a price. We can be now here and later there, but never both here and there simultaneously.

We can't go out to a nightclub without wondering what's
happening at home, nor stay home while also being part of
the nightclub festivities. In fact, within our own bodily make-
up we find a dispersal in space that is often frustrating and
sometimes tragic. Our bodies are extended in space, so that
parts are outside of parts, one part here and the other there.
And so, we cannot scratch our right elbow with our right
hand. And sometimes we cannot reach a brake pedal in time
to avert a collision, because certain brain centers are simply
too distant from the muscles that they command.

All of these limitations – specific, individual, temporal
and spatial – constitute our finitude, our existential or ontological loneliness and solitude. Our very existence is limited,
restricted, cut off from that of other beings. Each one of us
must say, "Yes, I do exist, and I am human. I am myself,
here and now." And all of that existential fullness is real, and
wonderful, and precious – infinitely better than not existing
at all. But each of us must also say, with varying degrees
of regret, "But I am only human, only myself, only here,
and only now." Those "only's" constitute our existential or
ontological loneliness. That loneliness is not always felt; we
are at times scarcely aware of it as we go about our business
within existential limits that we take for granted. But at
times we feel lonely, too. And then our ontological loneliness
is redoubled by a psychological loneliness. We know ourselves
to be lonely, finite, separate from the rest of men and from
the vast universe as well. We feel discomfort, frustration,
even anguish, at times, when that deeper loneliness comes to
our conscious mind. But the deeper, ontological loneliness
remains a constant fact whether we are aware of it or not,
whether we feel it or not. As individual beings among a multitude, we are, in our very existence, solitary, diverse, each of
us alone, i.e., "all one," entirely one and not the others.[17]

Human activities, like the activities of all other such finite beings, spring out of a natural, pre-conscious desire to
remedy this ontological loneliness. All beings other than God
seek to extend, expand, increase their existential perfection,
their very existence, by reaching out, forming links of various kinds with other finite beings. All seek to transcend
themselves in some fashion, to keep their original being even
while reaching out to posssess the reality of other beings. All

---

[17] Jean Mouroux, *The Meaning of Man* (Garden City: Doubleday and Co., Inc.,
1961), pp. 65-81.

action, then, including the actions of human beings seeking
to build community, are rooted in a radical self-seeking, a
drive to overcome finitude in any and all possible ways. At
root, finite beings act out of a drive to possess, somehow, the
existence of the other solitary individuals around them, to
communicate in being, to become one with each other. Thus
elements form compounds, plants and animals absorb nutri-
ents, animals move around, sense their environment, reproduce themselves. We humans also nourish ourselves, grow,
reproduce, sense, and move around. But our distinctively human way of overcoming solitude is psychological. We enter
into unity with, share the existence of, other beings through
knowing and loving them. With our minds and wills, we can
transcend time and space, we can be more than just ourselves; we can transcend our own individuality. We can be,
all at once, both human and more. We can be both ourselves
and others. We can be both here and there, both now and
then. And one of these modes of self-transcendence constitutes community, in which our entire concrete existence, with
no detriment to its original integrity, comes to be one with
the entire concrete existence of the rest of the universe.

But let us look first at one of our lesser modes of self-
transcendence, cognition. Something mysterious happens in
every act of our mind, every time we become conscious of
something other than ourselves. We have the reality or existence of what we know within us, in our minds. When I hear
a bird, see a sunset, conceive an idea or make a judgment,
I have that bird or sunset, that object conceived or judged,
within my mind. And yet, what I know continues to exist,
unchanged, in its full integrity, outside my mind. Nor has
my mind lost its identity, its existential integrity as a being
separate from its object. Two beings, knower and known,
have become one without ceasing to be two. In cognition, we
achieve community of a certain basic kind (though not the
kind that is the main thesis of this book). When I know anything, then, I transcend myself. I go beyond myself without
leaving myself behind. I experience a net gain, an increase of
my very being, for I come to be that which I know. To have
within me the reality of a bird or a sunset is, in some important sense, to be a bird or a sunset without ceasing to be a
person, indeed, without ceasing to be the individual person
that I am.

This understanding of human cognition is not original in
medieval philosophy, of course. Long before that the Greeks
had held that the perfection of man, his ontological perfec-

tion, consists in having the entire universe contained within
him, through knowledge. Mere consciousness, rooted in a
drive to perfect ourselves, allows a certain healing of our ontological loneliness. Am I only human? But I can be that
and more, simply by knowing other things, other natures,
other essences. Am I only myself, alone in a crowd of other
human beings? I can be myself and others, too, thanks to
imagination, to memory, to intimacy. As children, we said
it well: "You be the teacher and I'll be the student." "It's
my turn to be the policeman today – you got to be one yes-
terday." "I had you on my mind all day." "I can't come
to your party, but I'll be with you in spirit." Cognition is
a mysterious stretching of our minds, and thus an extension
of our selves, into other times and places, into other persons
and things. Have I lost my childhood by becoming an adult?
But I can still have it, cherish it, enjoy it, even enhance it –
in my memory. And I can be in two places at once, or even
more, as I sit in my chair and fantasize a beach, a bar, an
Alpine peak. Who hasn't said, usually apologetically, "Sorry,
I didn't hear you. I was 1000 miles away"?

This overcoming of our finitude, the healing of our ontological loneliness through cognition, may seem like small
comfort, indeed. But it is infinitely better than no self-
transcendence at all. A rock or a plant is condemned to
be, always, just what it is – this individual of this kind, here
and now. Animals, who share sense perception with us – and
some of them memory and imagination as well – are somewhat better off, able to live in the past, dream of a future
meal, and so on. But no other being in nature can transcend
itself as we do. The evidence for our distinctively human
power to heal our ontological loneliness is the fact of human
history, the development of civilization. We alone among
the animals have a history, a story of progress that could
only have come about through self-reflective intelligence. It
is only because we are able not only to know but also to know
that we know, able to criticize the knowledge that we have
and search for the knowledge that we don't have, that we
humans have been able to move out of an original primitive
mode of life to the urbanity of modern civilization. History is
there, no mean achievement. And it is there because we can
know, and can invent symbols for sharing what we know with
each other. The value of our self-transcendence in cognition,
then, is the value of history itself, the value of civilization. It

is there for all to see.[18]

And yet, civilization is not the whole story. Social contract theory can, and does, give a plausible account of civilization, as does a philosophy of community. But community is not to be identified with civilization. Civilization, indeed, taken in its totality or its various segments, could well be anti-communal. It has the potential to be communal as well, though, and so some further distinctions are in order. Do we wish, for example, to count the development of nation-states locked in a suicidal nuclear stalemate as an instance of our race's steady progress? Is our current society, with rapidly rising numbers of divorces, abortions, and children living in poverty what we have in mind when we say *community*? How is it that people can live in community and feel deep emotional anguish, as did, say, some of the inmates of Hitler's death camps? What should we say about their jailers, on the other hand, who enjoyed a quiet camaraderie as they went about their murderous business? Is shared joy, the intimacy of shared thoughts and feelings, the same as community? Why do black people seem to resent references to "the black community," even when those references are benevolent? And how is it that a couple may live in great physical closeness, sharing a house and a bed, sharing thoughts and feelings, and still feel a desperate loneliness? The lines between ontological and psychological loneliness, ontological and psychological healing, physical closeness and personal communion have to be more clearly marked.

The best way to understand these distinctions is to look at the make-up of the human person, and then to see how various elements of that make-up are involved in different kinds of distance and different kinds of closeness. We are strange and wonderful composites of matter and spirit, with matter accounting for our limitations or finitude – our individuality, our space-time limits. "Spirit" names our ability to reach beyond these material limits, through the immaterial powers of mind and will, our capacities for thinking and for loving altruistically. In between these elements of our make-up, partly material and partly immaterial, are our senses and emotions – memory, imagination, joy, sadness, anger, and so on. Thanks to all these various components, we can find our-

---

[18] See Aquinas' *Summa Theologiae*, I, 14, 1, "On Whether There is Knowledge in God?" for the metaphysics which makes cognition an expansion of the knower's existence. Mouroux develops the thesis in Chapter VI, "The Human Person." (*The Meaning of Man*, pp. 113-129).

selves in quite different states of loneliness and fulfillment.

The fundamental loneliness is the finitude, or ontological loneliness, already described – our humanity, our individuality, our space-time limitations. This fundamental loneliness is a constant fact, whether we advert to it or not. It is due, in the final analysis to the multiplicity of being. The act of existing is really multiplied, so that each being has its own. Beings, then – not just human beings, but all others as well – are diverse, separate from each other, not part of each other or of some underlying unified "stuff" that constitutes the world. We are really many units, many beings. And so shall we always be. There is no ontological healing that can overcome this ontological loneliness in its own order. For any sharing of existence which would overcome the diversity and multiplicity of our being would change our original identities. As the husband on "United States" said, "Only one of us can be me." If two persons or any other two beings were to merge ontologically so as to exist by one and the same act of existence, they would no longer be two beings, but one. And then one would lose his identity and his existence. When a missionary is eaten by a cannibal, he doesn't exist in him afterwards. He doesn't exist at all. Rather than two becoming one, one has ceased to exist, and the other continues to exist as before, his original solitude intact.[19]

This fundamental and persistent loneliness or diversity is due, in Aquinas' view, to the metaphysical make-up of the human person, to the structure by which we are real existents. Each of us has several components in a complex structure of matter and spirit that accounts for all the predicates that we can assign to any given person. Thus, I can say, "I am human, white, female, green-eyed, a wife, a professor, a mother," and so on. The totality of my structure, the concrete individuality by which I am unique in all the world, is expressed by my name. But the single most important feature of my total make-up is my act of existence, that actuality which enables me to say, "I am. I exist as a real, actual person, not just as a possibility, a character in fiction, a gleam in my father's eye." The act of existing is fundamental to the make-up of a person much as a foundation is fundamental – foundational – to a house. Existence "supports,"by actualizing or making

---

[19] A famous line of Aristophanes' to this effect is quoted by Aquinas in his treatise on love, at *S.Th.* I-II, 28, 1, "Whether Union is an Effect of Love?" St. Thomas is quoting Aristotle's quotation of Aristophanes. The theme is a commonplace in philosophical discussions of friendship and community.

real, all the other components. And so, to remove the act of existing from a person would be analogous to removing the foundation from a house – all the rest would collapse in ruins. Existence, though, is even more foundational than a foundation. To take away a person's act of existing would cause the rest of the person not just to collapse in ruins, but to vanish into non-being or nothingness. Remove my act of existing, and you remove my very self – my humanity, my individuality, my very presence in time and space.[20]

How, then, does cognition heal our ontological loneliness? In our thoughts and judgements, we enjoy or possess the reality of whatever object we are thinking of. It takes up its existence in our minds even as it stays intact in the world. We exercise the existence of a bird or a sunset even as we continue to exercise our own human existence. There is no loss of existence here, but rather a net gain. This increase of a knower's being comes about through images, concepts and other mental representations of the things he knows. In other words, he exercises their existence vicariously, indirectly, through the medium of representative images of them in his mind. Thus, when I "be" a teacher as a child playing school, I am both a child and a teacher, but not in exactly the same way. I am a child really, existentially, metaphysically, by my own personal act of existing. I am a teacher mentally, intentionally, psychologically by the representative image of a teacher in my mind. My ontological loneliness is healed psychologically, by a mental rather than a real communion with what I know, through the medium of various images existing in my mind while intending the real.

But the ontological loneliness that is a constant of human existence persists even in our cognitional communion with the things and people that we know. No matter what I know, what I am in my mental world, I am still, in reality, only human, only myself, only in this place at this time. Friendship brings a deeper, better healing. For an affective, felt loneliness is sometimes an important part of our awareness of ourselves. Sometimes, in addition to being lonely, we know that we are and feel lonely as well. This mood or feeling of loneliness is more intense at some times than at others. But it is nothing more than an awareness of, and emotional response to, the ontological loneliness that is our fundamen-

---

[20] See Johann, *The Meaning of Love*, pp. 56-68. He is using Aquinas to make the point.

tal condition. This second kind of loneliness, psychological loneliness, also has a certain psychological healing. When we are in communion with beings other than ourselves – other persons, perhaps, or things in nature – we often know that we are and take comfort and delight in that knowledge. Then we not only <u>are</u> less alone, but feel that way, too. This psychological healing may be merely cognitional – the communion, in our minds, that we mentioned above. That intentional, contemplative union is genuine enough. But it may bring emotional satisfaction with it as well. We sometimes delight in what we contemplate. That delight can be especially intense, as in aesthetic experience. Poets have described the joy of being at one with nature. This delightful contemplative or cognitional union reaches a certain high point in those human relationships that we call intimate. Spouses or old friends who know each other well, who have an easy and ongoing dialogue in which they share each other's thoughts and feelings, often experience one of the keenest delights, one of the deepest emotional satisfactions known to man.

Both ontological and psychological loneliness, then, are healed when people come to know each other and to take delight in their intimacy. But intimacy is not community. For that, we must look to another healing, one that is more direct and immediate than the indirect union of cognition, mediated as it is by concepts and other mental images of the ones we contemplate. This further healing, which brings people into real, existential rather than merely cognitional, communion, is the altruistic love that generates community. Thanks to the difference between knowing and loving, between mind and will, cognitional union – wondrous as it is – is not the full story. Thanks to our power to love altruistically, to identify with another person as our other self, we can construct a bond between us by which we really, not just mentally, possess a beloved's act of existence as our own. We are then in union with that beloved person's whole being, in a union that is immediate and total, direct and real. When I pretend to be a teacher, or come to know the mind of an intimate friend, I am that other person mentally, as I possess certain thoughts and ideas which make him present within myself. But when I love one of my teachers, or an intimate friend, I possess that beloved person's very existence, and hence his total reality as a person, as my own. Instead of drawing him into myself, as I do in contemplating him, I extend myself outward toward his entire being, identifying it as my own. Love has about it a realism that cognition never enjoys, even that special kind of cognition known as intimacy. Let us look at this astonishing process of identification again.

The key to understanding identification is the difference between the intentionality of a mind and the realism of a will. The term *identify* means, in its Latin roots, "to make the same as." When I identify another as my other self, I make him the same as my self. The process combines moral imagination with effective willing, and has three distinct elements, each of them necessary if community is to come about. First, in looking upon another as my other self, I recognize his humanity. I take him as my exact equal, neither more nor less. His human dignity, his worth as a person, his human rights are exactly equivalent to my own. I neither look down on him as my inferior, nor up to him as my superior. I don't manipulate, seduce, or terrorize him. Nor do I toady to him, grovel before him, or idolize him. A lover makes his beloved his exact equal. But I do not just look upon him as another human, as any other whatsoever, as a self other than my own self. He is my other self, somehow belonging to me, linked to me, in some sort of unity.

Once I recognize him as my other self, I move into the second moment of identification, in which I wish for that beloved other self what I would wish for myself if I were that other person. I offer him not just my acknowledgement of his equal humanity, but a concern equal to what I have for myself. And yet, that concern is for him in his otherness, not for me. If I'm going to give him a gift, for example, I will give him something appropriate to his needs or tastes, not what I myself would like. In other words, I don't make him the same as me, but make me the same as him. In this moment of identification, I need to use my moral imagination. I must try to see the world as he does, "walk in his moccasins." I must imagine what it is like to be that other person, and try to discern what is good for him precisely as the person he is, as someone other than myself, as my other self. Respect for the loved one's individuality is thus built into community right from the beginning. In this basic, foundational act of identification, all possibilities that community might threaten or diminish the individual uniqueness of its members are simply precluded. Just as the first moment of identification guarantees total respect for the beloved's human dignity and human rights, so does this second moment assure respect for his individuality, which the lover cherishes as deeply as his own.

This decentering of the lover's concern, from his original self to his other self, implies the third and most crucial element of the identification which constitutes community. Having taken another as my other self, and having wished for him what I would wish for myself if I were he, I must wish that good to him for his sake rather than my own. And here is the deepest, as well as the most important, paradox in our philosophy of community. For while all actions of all finite beings originate in a kind of self-seeking, as efforts to overcome their ontological loneliness, a person who would heal his loneliness by partaking in community with another must not be motivated by his own need for such healing. The healing will come, and he will welcome it. But it will come only as a side-effect of his concern for his other self. I must love my friend, and seek to be joined to him, not for any good that accrues to me in the process, but solely for the sake of the good that accrues to him as my other self. Otherwise the realism of my will will make community impossible. Where my will is, there is myself. And in egocentric motives, my will is within my original self.

The key to love as a communion which heals our onto-logical loneliness, in a more realistic way than does cogni-tion, is located right here. When I identify another's good as my own, precisely as his good, for his sake, I really make his good my own. The paradoxical reality of community, in which many become one without ceasing to be many, results from this process of identification. For in this process, we truly make the good of another our own, even as we leave it intact as the good of another. We simply choose to take that good as our own, to be concerned for it, and in so doing, in and by that choice, we make it ours. Willing is not wishful thinking. It is, rather, real efficiency. I don't merely pretend that my beloved's good is my own. I make it mine, effectively and really, in and through my altruistic love.

The psychological process of identification thus has on-tological effects, for will is a realistic power rather than an intentional one. When I identify with a friend in altruistic love, we come to possess a single good in common. The point is subtle, but all-important. We are not saying, for example, that if I wish well to another person, I will be rewarded, be-cause he will return his love to me. (Students often make this mistake. One came to my office one day, flushed with enthusiasm, and said, "Prof, you are really right about al-truistic love. I've been trying it for three weeks now, and it really works.") In the first place, love is not always recip-rocated. But even when it is, it is not the reciprocity that constitutes the communion. When I give someone an album,

for example, as an act of altruistic love, the single good that
the two of us possess in common is precisely my friend's pleasure in hearing the music. That pleasure is obviously his, for
he feels it. It is part of his ontological structure as a person.
But that very same pleasure is mine also, even if I do not enjoy the music, because I choose to make my friend's pleasure
my good, in my identification with him. True, I might also
feel my own pleasure in the music. But that feeling, too, is
beside the point. My pleasure is not the tie that binds, but
a side-effect of the binding. What binds us together as one is
the fact that one and the same good, the one that I wish to
my beloved, belongs to both of us. The pleasure that he feels
is his because he feels it. And that very pleasure is mine also
simply because I choose to look upon it, and to will it, as my
good. In this case, I have caused it, labored to bring it into
being. As Aristotle said, the effects that I cause are an extension of my very being. But in other cases, too – moments
of various kinds of loveplay, where I do nothing for my friend
but simply enjoy the good that is already there, willing that
good to him for his sake – my being also extends into him,
making his existence my existence as well. The fulfillment of
his self is identically the fulfillment of my self, simply because
I have willed it to be so. Such is the power of altruistic love.

Paradoxically, the two of us remain two in this communion. Neither of us is diminished in the separate, individuated selves that we were prior to our communion. And yet
we are one with each other in our joint possession of a single
good. And it is this possession of the good of another that
constitutes a fulfillment, a healing of ontological loneliness,
for the one who loves altruistically. The fulfillment for the
one who is loved is obvious enough – my friend gets a new album, and feels a pleasure that he would not have felt without
my gift. What is less obvious but of crucial importance for
community is that the lover is also fulfilled, precisely in his
giving. His ontological good is increased, his finitude tran-
scended, because he now claims the good of another – the
good of his other self – as his own. He is no longer the solitary individual, limited to being only himself, that he was
before he loved. His ontological loneliness is healed in and
through his own loving, whether it is reciprocated or not. Altruism brings a psychological healing to ontological loneliness
that is real, unlike the mental healing found in cognition.[21]

The built-in increase of an altruistic lover's being is now

---

[21] Such is the conclusion of Aquinas' argument that love is both unitive (drawing
the beloved into the lover) and ecstatic (moving the lover into communion with the

evident. Moderns tend to think of altruism as a kind of
self-abandon, a way of giving up our own welfare in favor of
the welfare of others. But it is, in fact, quite the reverse.
Altruism is the only way to self-fulfillment, to extending our
own existence, to transcending our built-in limitations. It
is our only way to say, "Now I am no longer just myself,
only here, only now. I am also you, also there and then, but
without ceasing to be myself, here and now." A lover has two
selves, even, as we shall see, more than two. But his altruistic
motivation remains crucial. For as soon as he makes his own
fulfillment his motive, seeking his fulfillment for his own sake,
he loses out on the communion that could fulfill. In seeking
his healing directly, he loses it. For while self-seeking is the
root of his action, when it becomes his conscious motive,
he fails to identify with his beloved. He does not then see
him as his other self, does not seek what is good for him,
does not seek it for his beloved's sake. His will is fixed on
his own solitary well-being. And so, that reinforced solitude
is the only possible outcome of his action. His ontological
loneliness is reinforced by the fixing of his will on his solitary
self instead of on his other self.

The reverse side of the paradox is thus evident, too.
While it might seem that the way in which to find my fulfillment is to seek it, to make it the purpose and goal of my
actions, the opposite is really the case. For once I approach
others with an eye to my own welfare and fulfillment, my
entire view of them changes. I do not see them as my other
selves, equal in dignity and in human rights. I see them as inferior to myself, as means to my ends. They are appendages
to my self rather than other selves in their own right. My attention and concern are then egocentric, not decentered from
my original, ontologically lonely self. Since that is the case,
I do not even try to "walk in their mocassins," nor to discern
what is good for them. My moral imagination is fully occupied with my own, egocentric well-being. Finally, I do not
wish any good to others for their sakes. I arrogate to myself,
for my sake, the good of others. The result is not ontological healing, but a reinforcement of my original finitude. I
possess no good in common with my fellows. I come into no
communion with them. My quest for my own fulfillment has
defeated itself.

---

beloved precisely as other than himself). The two movements of love are not contraries,
but, rather, enhance each other. Love is unitive by virtue of being ecstatic.

This double paradox is clearly exemplified in the two parents, with their differing relationships to their son, in the recent Academy Award winning movie, *Ordinary People*. One scene showed quite clearly that the father, Calvin, loved his son altruistically. The boy told his father that he was entering into psychotherapy, and that it would cost a lot of money. The father told him not to worry. He had, in fact, long wanted his son to get the therapy he needed, for the sake of the boy's mental health. When that new health came about, Calvin, the father, could claim it as his good, too, because he had identified his son's well-being as his own. He found fulfillment for himself in communion with his son, as a side-effect of his concern for his son's mental health. In another scene, however, the mother exemplified just as clearly the self-defeat of an egocentric concern. When her son dropped his membership on the swimming team, the mother, Beth, was very upset. She was upset because she lost prestige among her friends, not because she saw any good for her son in his being on the team. In fact, she was depicted throughout the movie as having no concern for her son's well-being at all. She never even thought about what was good for him. Her motivation was almost entirely self-centered. The movie rightly portrayed her, then, as a more tragic figure than her son. For in seeking her own fulfillment directly, she caused it to slip from her grasp. Her husband told her as much, in the poignant scene of their parting, when he said, "I wonder if you have ever really loved anybody."

Community, then is a psychological reality, an act of will that constructs a tie that really binds. But this mode of healing ontological loneliness is real, not just intentional. And without altruistic identification, one person has no share in another's existence. Egocentric associates, even if they enjoy a most exquisite intimacy, remain closed within their ontological solitude. There may be many pairings and groupings of people, then, that may look like communities but are not. They may be intimacies, societies, associations or nations, but not communities at all. They may bring people into physical and even cognitional closeness, but not into real community. When such associations claim to be, or seem to be, communities, they are mere counterfeits. Social scientists, for example, would wish to call any group of people living together and sharing common interests and projects a community. By that definition, geographic and political units are all communities. Thus we could legitimately speak of Chicago as a community, and Canada as well. The Brinks

robbers were a community, as were all those who collaborated
with the Third Reich. We can even speak of the college community, the business community, the medical community, the
gay community, the black community, the community of the
Third World.

But if altruistic love is the tie that binds, then we have
to ask the all-important question about motivation before
we dignify a group or a pair with the title *community*. Mere
physical closeness, being in the same place at the same time,
does not produce any psychological communion between people. Thus the members of some gathering such as a city or a
country, a family, an audience, may or may not be a community, depending on the motives which bring them together.
Businessmen who act out of the profit-motive and in competition with each other are seeking to maximize profits at
each other's expense, a multitude of egocentric individuals,
not really united at all except, perhaps, in time and space.
On the other hand, people who are far apart in time and
space – spouses who are separated by their work, for example – may be in very real communion with each other, if only
one of them loves the other altruistically.

Community, then, is not the same as physical closeness,
though it may bring people together in time and space. When
we love, we reach out and touch someone – perhaps only with
a loving will, perhaps through some technique of communication such as the long distance telephone as well. Ideally, those
who love do associate with each other, speak to each other,
embrace, spend time together, engage in common projects.
Surely a community which is also a close association has a
kind of richness that community dispersed in time and space
would lack. The ideal is to love and associate as well, to
have both community and closeness. But if we must choose,
then community without association is better than association without community because it is real, not illusory, communion.

But why should real communion be so important? Because only real communion can heal our radical, ontological
loneliness. When we love altruistically, community is our
ontological healing, a transcendence of our own existential
limits, a fulfillment of the emptiness of our existential solitude. Sometimes community is an emotional healing as well,
an association that feels good. But when we love, we acquire
an ontological good that is real and existentially fulfilling,
even when the communion brings emotional pain and hardship. The parents who care for a severely handicapped child,

for example, find their ontological fulfillment in so doing, as surely as do the parents who have the joy of an intimate lifetime with a healthy and active child. A community that is emotionally fulfilling, in which friends of the third kind are also useful and pleasant to each other, is surely richer in some important sense than one that is marked by pain and hardship. But again, if we must choose, then community takes priority over familiarity and romance, over utility and pleasure. In short, our best state is a community that is also joyous. The best friendships are based on the virtue of love, but include utility and pleasure as well. But love without utility, love without pleasure, is better than both utility and pleasure without love. For love makes community real. Ontological healing without emotional fulfillment is better than emotional fulfillment without ontological healing. Community is our highest good, because nothing else increases our very being. Community, and nothing else, makes us more real than we are without it.

CHAPTER III

COMMUNITIES AND CONTRACTS

Community, then, is an interior regime, an affective reality. A community of two (or more, as we shall see in Chapter IV) exists in the mind and heart of each and every person who loves anyone altruistically. For such love binds the existence, and thus the entire concrete reality, of a beloved to his lover. Communities may also be societies or associations. That is, those who are united in love may also be close to each other in time and space, sharing experiences and activities, and undertaking common projects. They may be intimates. When a community is enacted in loving outward associations, it takes on a new richness that is entirely appropriate to its human members, composites, as they are, of matter and spirit. Love is fundamentally a psychic reality, and may be nothing more. A community that is not an association is a real community for all that. But a community that is also an association is more humanly complete, for it involves action as well as contemplation, body as well as mind, emotion as well as will.

Contractual connections, on the other hand, can only be societies or associations, never communities. Contracts, inherently egocentric in their motivation, can only link people in their external aspects. Contracts can bring people together in the same place at the same time, to share a common activity or project. But since those who love contractually are seeking their own fulfillment as their end, looking to other people as the means to their own pleasure or utility, they forge no existential bonds with each other. Since each self keeps his will fixed on his own self, the good of that self is all that he really possesses. He fails to unite with the existence of another, thanks to his fundamental indifference to that existence. And in so doing, he fails to unite with any of the metaphysical structure of that other. Contracts produce associations only, never communities. And those associations are abstract, not existential.

One paradoxical implication of this conclusion is that one and the same group, society, friendship, marriage or other association may be a community for one or several of its members and not for others. Those who love the other members altruistically are in community with them. But those who love egocentrically are only associated with the others, not united to them in any personally real way. A marriage, then, can be a real tie that binds one spouse to another, and a sham which merely associates the other with the one. Probably what happens in most human associations, especially those which last for any length of time, is that community becomes episodic. That is, without any discernible change in our outward behavior, we move into community with our fellows and then out of it, in a rhythm of wavering motives. We love altruistically for a while, and thus enjoy community, only to lapse into selfishness and thus fall from a communal to a merely social life together. Community lasts as long as altruistic love lasts, and no longer.

As an example, compare two donors to a charity – say, the Jerry Lewis Telethon. Both may seem to be doing the same action, especially two who donate the same amount of money and thus finance identical operations, with identical results, for two different crippled children. But if we look beyond these outward actions to the inner motives from which they spring, our two donors could be existentially quite different from each other. Suppose one of them gives his money out of genuine concern for the well-being of the children, a well-being that he altruistically identifies as his good, also. This donor will receive many benefits to himself – free advertising, a tax advantage, and not least, community with the children. Their improved health and mobility are his goods, too, provided he maintains his altruistic motivation. But let his purity of heart falter, so that his reason for giving the money becomes his own financial advantage, or even his own ontological fulfillment in community, and community instantly ceases. Purity of heart is absolutely necessary for community to exist, for anyone who would partake of it. We must will one thing only – the good of the beloved, for the beloved's sake.

As long as our donor loves the children for their sakes, however, he is in community with them, and that community is a fact whether he ever associates with them or not. He may never come to know them. They may never come to know him. They may never thank him, offer reciprocal love, or even know who he is. He still finds community with them, through the psychological bond by which he links his will to their welfare. And in his community with them, he finds his ontological loneliness healed. Perhaps he will, some day, begin to associate with them. Perhaps he will become their friend, even an intimate friend. In that case, their community will also be an association. And perhaps he will find immense emotional rewards in that friendship, so that his emotional loneliness is healed as well. Then community reaches its high point. For then it is both interior communion and exterior closeness, both ontological and psychological healing. Then our donor's fulfillment is real, and it feels good as well. He exists beyond the boundaries of his own spatio-temporal individuality, and feels joy in doing so.

Our second donor, on the other hand, is motivated by crass business concerns. His name will be mentioned on national television, a bit of advertising that he calculates to be worth more than the donation that is its price. His personal prestige will go up even as his taxes go down. And these financial benefits to himself, along with his enhanced prestige and feelings of self-esteem, constitute his reason for making his donation. One result, of course, is that crippled children are enabled to have surgery that they wouldn't have otherwise, and they enjoy new health and new mobility as a result. But as far as our donor's motives are concerned, these benefits to the children are beside the point. They are not his good. For he does not identify those goods as his own, and does not wish them to happen to the children, for the children's sake.

This second donor, in contrast to the first, does not come into community with the children he helps, because his will, which could forge a bond with the good of others, remains centered on his own individual ego. Thus he finds no healing of his ontological loneliness, whether he later associates with the children or not. The best he can achieve is an association which is not a community, an emotional healing which is a sham because it has no underlying ontological healing. Suppose our second donor does become a friend of the children he helps. Suppose he spends time with them, so that they and he get to know each other, to enjoy each other's company, to be together in time and space and shared activities. As far as the donor is concerned, their association is only that, an association – but not a community. He may find immense emotional rewards, a true pleasure in his association with the children. He may feel less lonely than before. But he will be as lonely as ever, locked into the boundaries of his own spatio-temporal individuality because of his fixing his will on his own ego.

The point may seem subtle, a psychological triviality, but it is not. Community is a psychological reality, and our motives determine whether it happens or not. In matters of human actions and interactions, psychological realities are ontological as well. When we speak of the second donor's selfishness as being self-defeating, as frustrating his quest for

his own fulfillment, we do not mean that he will experience
pangs of regret, that his selfishness will drive away his friends,
that he is missing out on the joys of reciprocal love. All
of these emotional states may or may not happen, and all
are beside the point. The point is that his psychological
state – his fixation of his will on his own welfare – makes his
ontological fulfillment impossible. For him, no matter what
other costs and benefits may weigh in the picture, community
does not exist. He is existentially less than he might be. And
that foundational frustration is a fact, whether he adverts to
it or not, whether he feels it or not.

Social contract theory originated, with thinkers of the
Enlightenment, as an effort toward community. But its emphasis has always been on a radical individuality – on individual rights, individual freedom, individual fulfillment.
Community – especially political community, but other associations as well – has been said to come about by agreements,
contracts, negotiations, whether explicit or tacit. The purpose of all such associations is the protection of the rights and
the freedom of individuals. Thus the person as an atomic,
detached individual is prior to his relations and associations
with others. In our natural condition, we are not just individuals, however. We are individuals in competition and conflict
with each other, our natural state Hobbe's "war of all against
all." The protection of individual rights and freedoms is not
the protection of all individuals, but only each individual ego.
I protect my rights, you protect yours, and we protect each
other's only as a means to protecting our own. Human associations, then, even when they are the product of various
social contracts, are essentially power struggles. Conflicts between persons are seen as conflicts of rights. And conflicts are
settled by negotiation and renegotiation, processes in which
each party gives up some of his individual freedom and some
of his individual rights in order to preserve the rest. The
way to solve all problems concerning the associations of individuals with each other is the cost-benefits analysis that our
second donor to the Jerry Lewis Telethon typifies.

Social contract theory thus mandates egocentric motives
in all interactions between human beings. For the valuing of
the individual, endowed with sacred rights and the freedom
to pursue them, is not an equal valuing of all individuals, nor
even a selective valuing of only some individuals. Rather,
social contract theory has turned out to be a valuing of this
individual above all others – the individual speaking, the first
person pronoun, the I. Each individual gives primacy to his

own private self. With such egoism, there is no love of others for their sakes, no identification of their good as one's own. The egoism built into the assumptions behind a contractual view of human relations precludes community because it precludes the tie that binds. The end result has not been happy. We need only to think of the devastating wars in our century, the nuclear arms race, the willingness of the United States to go to war again to protect a life-style based on the petroleum that is a natural resource of the Middle East. Smaller societies, such as families and friendships, have hardly been remarkable for their stability and happiness in modern times. The reason is that our guiding theories, the variations on the theme of social contract thought, do not show us how to end the war of all against all, by turning it into a community of all with all, a love of all for all. We merely restrain that war, leaving its individualistic egoism alive and well just below the surface.

Our failures to achieve community are not just practical ones, due to imperfect techniques of government and social organizing. Nor are they due merely to human weakness or the imperfections of our technology of communication. The failure of social contracts is intrinsic to them. The primacy of the individual ego requires egocentric motives for human interactions. Such motives make community impossible in advance, because they preclude the identification which brings people together in a joint possession of common good.

Aristotle anticipated the fatal flaw of social contracts in his analysis of friendships of the first two kinds. The flaw is present at their core, even when we put such associations in their best possible light. Friends who find each other useful, for example, wish well to each other and do right by each other. They treat each other justly, and may be friends for a long time. Their constant collaboration on common goals and common projects makes them congenial and they may even come to enjoy each other. But sooner or later, they break up. Such friends become competitive and begin to quarrel. They don't always understand their agreements in the same way, and so their expectations are often disappointed. They frequently disagree about what constitutes a just exchange between them, even when they put their agreements in writing. The tendency to become rivals rather than friends is intrinsic to their association, because that association is rooted in inequality – each needs something that the other has and has something that the other needs.

Friendships of the second kind, those based on pleasure,
are somewhat more alluring. But they are contracts, too.
Such friends associate with each other because they find delight in the same goals and easily agree on the means to those
goals. Their mutual delight leads them to be generous with
each other rather than competitive. These friends do not experience the quarrels and disagreements typical of those who
cling together for utility's sake. They don't calculate what
they give to each other, and are not so often disappointed
in their expectations. Their feelings of delight tend to make
their friendship smoother and more enduring.[22]

We can almost read in this description of Aristotle's
friendships of pleasure a picture of the casual sexual liaisons
held up as models in our contemporary culture. Couples pair
off on the basis of mutual pleasure, and sometimes make remarkable adjustments which lead to some stability in their
unions. Some such couples even have a sense of responsibility
for each other's welfare and for the children born to them.
Many marriages that are widely thought to be happy and
successful follow this pattern rather closely. How could anyone object to, say, a family in which the parents are linked in
mutual delight, enjoy sexual compatibility, share many common projects – notably the rearing of their children – and
live together peaceably for many years?

Such pairings seem, at first glance, to be infinitely better than partnerships based on utility. And yet, in the final
analysis, they are not. Both are counterfeits of community,
and both are so for the same reason. Their basis, the motivation of the friends, is the same in both: the egocentric
individualism that precludes community. Friends of utility
and of pleasure wish well to each other, but do so each for
his own sake, not that of the other. Their unity is abstract
rather than concrete, and thus not real. That is, their love
for each other is aimed not at each other's total selves, but
at some one feature that each finds useful or pleasant for
himself. And these qualities, mentally abstracted from the
concrete whole that is the other person, can weaken or die, or
can be found in a higher degree in someone else. Friendships
based on pleasure, then, may be somewhat more stable than

---

[22] Aristotle points to basic deficiencies in friendships of utility and pleasure, all
derived from fundamentally egocentric motives. Because such friends associate with
each other each for his own sake, their friendships are unstable, marked by volatility,
quarrels, and so on. See *Nichomachean Ethics*, VIII, 3, 1156a 10-20 and VIII, 4,
1157b, 1-5, for example.

those based on use, but in the final analysis, these are unstable, also. Marriages that have been happy and successful
for twenty-five years break up when one or the other spouse
loses his charm, or is replaced by a new person who comes on
the scene. For example, large hospitals where a great number
of mastectomies are performed have to offer counseling ses-
sions for wives who lose their husbands when they lose their
breasts. But there is a deeper point. Such friendships are
unstable because they are not communities to begin with.
They are, at best, alluring counterfeits of community that
make community impossible. They vitiate the love that is
the only tie that binds. Aristotle's first two kinds of friendship contain the fatal intrinsic flaw that was later to become
a central idea in social contract thought: the primacy of the
individual ego.

If self-transcendence in altruistic love is the distinctively
human way to ontological fulfillment, then all kinds of contractual relationships have to be ruled out as ways to genuine, as opposed to illusory, human fulfillment. The reason is
that contracts are intrinsically, and of necessity, egocentric.
And egocentric links with other people de-personalize them
in three basic ways. When I love someone with an eye to my
own fulfillment, whether it be ontological fulfillment, emotional joy, or both, I automatically make myself superior to
the other person instead of identifying him as my other self.
And when identification fails, so do altruism and community.
Such use of another person – and it is use even where pleasure is the motive, for it is my own pleasure that motivates
me – I degrade the other person in three basic ways. I turn
him into an object rather than a subject, into a means rather
than an end, and into a thing rather than a person. For example, when I isolate or abstract one quality from a person's
entire self, a quality which makes him useful or pleasant to
me, he becomes an object of my desire. I do not see him as
a subject, as a source of feeling and choices in his own right.
His personal dignity and needs are left out of the picture.
His uniqueness, then, disappears from the scene, too, and he
is reduced to the objectivity of one unit among many others
who have the same useful or pleasant quality.

To make someone an object rather than a subject is to
depersonalize him in a fundamental way. But the same attitude does even more. In seeing another merely in terms
of the pleasure or utility that he can yield for my needs, I
subordinate his welfare to my needs. He becomes a means to
my ends rather than an end in himself. For an end is that

which is loved for its own sake, for its own intrinsic goodness
rather than for some further good that it may lead to. A
mere means, on the other hand, lacks such intrinsic value.
Something that is valued as a mere means is valued not for
its own sake, but for the greater good to which it leads. Thus
using another person as a means to my own welfare – even
to my own ontological fulfillment – is to make my own good
the greater good, the end loved for its own sake. And then
the other person becomes a lesser good, devalued as a person
and loved only as a means.

The depersonalizing is complete, then. For someone who
is an object rather than a subject, and a means or relative
good rather than a absolute good loved for his own sake, is
no longer a person but a thing. Animals, plants, inanimate
objects like clothes, houses and automobiles are rightly used
for human pleasure and utility. Not being persons, they cannot be regarded as subjects, valued for their unique interior
realities, for they have none. Nor are these lesser beings absolute goods, treasured for their own sake, for the mere fact
of their existence. They exist in order to serve the needs
of higher, human beings. We rightly use them as means –
means to our own physical and emotional existence, comfort
and growth. But persons are beings of a different sort. Each
person is unique, and has an interior that is solely his own.
That interior consists of hopes, aspirations, the freedom to
love altruistically, the right to be so loved, the ability freely
to determine his own identity and fulfillment. Such unique
interiors are subjects, not objects, and thus are ends. Their
value is absolute. They are good in their own rights, simply
for being who they are. To objectify someone, then to make
him a means to anyone else's ends, is to rob him of his per-
sonhood. Since any contractual approach to a person does
precisely that, contractual relationships can never be communal. They are, by necessity, egocentric, thus abstractive,
and thus depersonalizing.[23]

Communal ties are the exact reverse, in every one of
these aspects. A friend of Aristotle's third kind wishes to
his beloved precisely what is good for that beloved as his
other self. He thus sees his friend as his own exact equal. He
treasures him as a subject – not as a mere object of the lover's

---

[23] Johann clearly shows how conditional love (thus contractual as opposed to communal association) depersonalizes the beloved. Conditions for love reduce the loved
one to the status of a means, an object, a thing, rather than respecting him as an end,
a subject, and a person. See *The Meaning of Love*, pp. 40-53.

desire and actions, but as someone with desires and needs, with thoughts and free decisions and hopes of his own. The altruistic lover cherishes in his beloved precisely this unique subjectivity. And in so doing, he values his beloved as an end rather than a mere means. He sees that other subjectivity, that other freedom and view of the world, that other center of activities, needs and hopes and dreams as something that is good in its own right. He values his beloved as an absolute good, good for what he is in himself, rather than as desirable only relatively, in terms of the lover's own needs for use and pleasure and ontological fulfillment. He loves his beloved for his beloved's own goodness, as an end, not as a mere means to some further good. Such friends are, of course, good for each other. They do fulfill each other, are useful to each other, and give each other pleasure. But all these relative goods, by which they are means, are secondary to the absolute good that each loves in the other as an end. Primarily, an altruistic lover sees it as a good that his friend exists, and is who he is, just in himself. He loves his friend's entire reality, not just an abstracted feature of it.

In so loving his beloved as a concrete whole, an altruistic lover does of course make his beloved an object – an object of his own desires and actions. But he is such an object only in a secondary way. Primarily, he is a subject, a source of activities of his own, with ideas, talents, a unique history and a unique future. Thus the altruistic lover does not reduce his beloved to the status of an object. He does not depersonalize him, treating his as a thing. His beloved is, in many ways, a means. He contributes to his lover's emotional and onto-logical fulfillment. But he is not merely a means. He is not even primarily that. First and foremost, he is who he is – a person, valued and loved as the lover's other self. He is an end in himself.

Contracts, then, because they are inherently egocentric in their motivation, are depersonalizing in their effects. Com-munal relationships, on the other hand, are inherently altru-istic in their motivation, and have as their effect the growth of persons precisely as persons. When I transcend myself by the altruistic love that begets community, I enhance myself precisely as a person in and through my communion with another, precisely as a person. There is a logic inherent in each of these two modes of interpersonal associations, a logic that holds even when we do not explicitly advert to it. As we explore this implicit logic, we can come to see a further, deeper difference between communities and contracts. The egocentric motivation that is essential to all contractual associations not only depersonalizes those who take part in such contracts. It includes, though usually in latent form, an ultimately murderous intent. And because of this murderous intent, such associations are not just unstable and illusory in the communion that they form. They bear within the deepest center of their members' hearts a willingness to destroy their members. A contrary logic is hidden in all communal relationships. For just as murder is the logical outcome of egocentric associations, so is self-sacrifice the logical outcome of altruistic love.

An example will help to make these two implicit logics explicit. Take a skilled manager who lacks the skills of a salesman, and have him form a partnership with a skilled salesman who lacks managerial talents. If the manager joins the salesman in a contract, he sees the salesman as one who, precisely in his business skills, is useful for supplying what the manager needs for making his business profitable. In truth, he may think no further about their relationship, may never examine his motives or ask whether their association is a true community or not. But there is a logic to this contract nonetheless. The logic may never become explicit, especially if the partnership runs smoothly and proves to be profitable for both of the partners. But if there is a crisis – a situation in which the relationship cannot continue as a contract, but must either become communal or break up – the logic will tell. And when it does, its ultimately murderous intent will out.

The relationship begins, and continues for a certain length of time, as a contractual one. The manager loves the salesman (wishes his welfare) for his own – the manager's – sake. He loves the salesman abstractly, for his salesmanship as an isolated trait. He has no explicit concern for his salesman's other features. He pays no attention to his political views, for example, except inasmuch as these might affect their business. He cares not about his family life, his childhood, his tastes in art and music, his athletic abilities, or his view of the world. He makes the salesman an abstraction, an object replaceable by any other skilled salesman. The salesman is, in the manager's eyes, a mere means, valued not for his own sake as an absolute good, but as instrumental to the company's profits. He is, in short, a thing rather than a person. Needless to say, the manager is not in communion with this salesman, but merely associates with him.

Such associations are common enough, of course, and
often quite congenial. The same pattern occurs in pairings
and groupings based on mutual pleasure. Partnerships, marriages, friendships, companies, military units, educational institutions, nations, alliances – all form and continue on the
basis of reciprocal egocentric motives. Many such associations are civilized, genteel, polite, and peaceable. They often
dissolve without becoming overtly homicidal. But their murderous intent is still present, even when it is latent and glossed
over by the conventions of civilized society and multitude of
gentlemen's agreements. For what is essential to any egocentric motivation is an indifference to the personal welfare of
the one who is loved. The members of such associations need
not wish any positive harm to each other. In fact, many of
them would be shocked and even outraged to hear that murderous intent lurks in their hearts. But it does. And in a
crisis, that murder will out. Anyone who is true to an original contractual motive, who follows wholeheartly the logic of
his self-primacy, will wish harm to his friend in a crisis. If a
situation should arise in which our manager's private welfare,
his profits, conflict with his salesman's personal well-being,
a contractual manager who is true to his deepest intentions
must do one of two things. He must either cling primarily
to his own private well-being as an atomic individual linked
only externally to his salesman, letting his friend's welfare
go by the boards. In that case, he follows the inherent logic
of all contractual associations. Or else he must be converted
to altruism. He must give up his egocentric self-primacy and
begin to love his friend for his friend's sake – as a subject, an
end, a person, as his other self. In that case, he frees himself
from the contract and enters into community. In short, their
association must either become communal or perish.

Suppose, for example, the salesman becomes seriously ill,
and can only be saved by a large contribution from the company's profits. A manager who is true to his egoism will keep
the profits and let his partner die. Business will be business,
after all. He will simply look for another salesman. Once
again, if he is true to his self-primacy, the logic of his egocentric ties to his friend gives him no motive for heroic refusal.
Many businessmen do resist, of course, just as many do dip
into their profits in order to save a partner's life. They are
inconsistent, violating the principle on which their association has been based. Fortunately, the logic of self-primacy
is rarely thought through in all its implications. Many egocentric contractors lack the consistency to follow their logic

through in action, once they become aware of its implications.

But that is exactly the point: those who do not follow through, those who do not consistently put profits ahead of personal concerns, are giving up the contract. Fortunately, the selfishness that is implicit in any contract does sufficiently horrify us when we become explicitly aware of it, so that we draw back from the abyss. But not all of us do. The Third Reich comes to mind, as do American segregationists and those who approve of our enjoyment of a high standard of living that is based on exploitation of the Third World. It is no accident that modern nation states, organized as they are on the basis of self-interest, have not been able to form even an apparent world community. War is a recurring threat. For it is but a small step from a hedonistic or utilitarian interest in the well-being of others to a cold indifference toward them. And it is but another step, smaller still, from indifference to competition, and from competition to outright murderous hostility. Let a crisis arise, and the logic of motives will tell.

The logic of community, with its altruistic motivation and ontological fulfillment of persons precisely as persons, is just as inevitable. But the conclusion of this logic is the reverse of murder: self-sacrifice, ultimately in the form of giving up one's life for a friend. To change our example, let us suppose our manager loves his salesman altruistically, welcoming his business skills but primarily wishing to him, for his sake, his welfare as a person. He loves the salesman, then, concretely, in his whole person rather than just for one isolated trait. This manager welcomes his salesman's initiatives and ideas, thus seeing him as a subject rather than just an object. He cares about his partner's health and family life, cherishes his hopes and memories, values his opinions on politics, art, music, his view of the world. He sees many benefits in his association with the salesman, not the least of which is his own ontological healing. But he is not motivated by these. He values his friend for his friend's sake, as an absolute good, good in his own right. He loves the salesman as an end, as the person that he is, unique in all the world. Such a manager lives in community with his partner.

Our altruistic manager may never advert to the logic of his position, but the logic is there, nevertheless. And the conclusion of the logic of altruism is self-sacrifice. A friend of the third kind who follows his altruistic intentions all the way to their logical conclusion may well find himself giving up his life for his friend, and doing so in utter certainty that it is good for him to do so. Many altruistic associations never

reach the point of such a demand, but the willingness to meet
it is implicit in everything that such friends wish and do for
each other. In many cases, partnerships like the one we have
described can go smoothly and pleasantly for long periods
of time, with both (or all) members taking joy in their hard
work together. Partners, spouses, friends make many sacrifices of time and energy, money and other material goods,
without any sense that they are doing so. The benefits of
their communion outweigh the costs. But let a crisis arise,
and the latent logic of their motives will tell. For what is
essential to this motivation is the very reverse of the egocentric motives of contracts. Instead of self-primacy, altruistic
unions are rooted in identification, in making each other each
other's other selves. What one gives over to the other, then,
is not given up, but given to one's other self, to become the
good that the two possess in common.

Whoever remains true to the logic of an original altruism, then, will gladly give up his life to save his friend in a
situation which demands such a gift. In a crisis, in which
he can either save his own life or support the well-being of
his friend, but not both, a friend of the third kind will continue through to the very end to support the well-being of
his friend. Suppose our altruistic manager can save his salesman's life only through an organ donation which will risk
his own life. He will risk his own life quite willingly, even if
the risk approaches 100%. Indeed, even if it were known to
be 100% – if he could save his friend from an oncoming car
only by stepping in front of it himself, say – he would do so
at once. The logic of his love demands the renunciation of
his own life, and rightly demands it in terms of his own fulfillment. A manager who would thus rescue his salesman at
the cost of his own life would be no masochist. His sacrifice
would be not so much a giving up as a giving over. For in
giving his life for his friend, he would find, if only he main-
tained his altruistic motivation, the fullest possible healing
of his own ontological loneliness. He would, by sacrifice, put
his total person at the service of, and thus in community
with, the entire person of his salesman. And his fulfillment
as a person, his ontological healing, would result. Community would become a fact whether there is an afterlife or not.
It would happen, and exist completely, in the moment of his
willingness to die for his friend.

Once we understand this point, we see where communities and contracts differ in a fundamental way. While community makes perfect sense of, and even logically demands,

self-sacrifice, contracts cannot justify it at all. In a contractual association – a business, a marriage, and international alliance – each member puts himself first and the other second, as a means to his use and pleasure. For such a one to give up his life for his friend, then, is fundamentally absurd. Any sacrifice is a giving up of one's own good in favor of the other, and thus defeats the purpose of the contract. Better to give up the association than to renounce one's self-primacy. But the height of absurdity, a masochism which makes no sense whatsoever, would be to give up one's life in order to save another. What good is that? How can one's death bring about one's own greater freedom, utility, pleasure, profits? Rather than dying for one's friend – who has suddenly lost his utility, since he is requiring his friend's life – the sensible thing is to take the friends's life in order to save his own. Egocentric love is intrinsically murderous.

But in a community, the reverse it true. Given his love of his friend as his other self, in whose welfare he finds his own ontological healing, one who loves altruistically makes the only sensible decision. Were our altruistic manager to refuse to give his own life in order to save his salesman, he would be acting against the logic of his love. Altruistic love fulfills the one who gives it by bringing him and the friend with whom he identifies into the common possession of a single good. Thus, the salesman's life is the manager's good. If the manager were, then, to cut himself off from the salesman's life by refusing to care for it, he would be reversing his altruistic love into selfishness. And that selfishness would defeat his ontological healing. For him, an egocentric clinging to his own life is the ultimate absurdity.

It may seem harsh to charge contractual associations with a murderous selfishness that is inherent to the motivation that sustains them. It may seem naive, or even self-serving, to credit communities with a self-sacrificing generosity that is inherent to the motivation that sustains them. But the analysis is not meant to impugn (or to praise) the motives of individuals in any personal way. The point has been that the ontology of community is established by a certain psychology on the part of its members, and the psychology of motives divides into two fundamentally incompatible views of the nature of the human person. In social contract terms, the self is a detached self, a solitary, atomic individual with no ties to other individuals. Ties have to be constructed, and the process of constructing them is a process of constant compromise. The good of others competes with the good of

the self, and so love of self competes with the love of others
as well. These two loves have to be repeatedly negotiated, for
egoism and altruism vary inversely. The love of one individual – the self – detracts from the love to another individual
– the friend. As one love increases, the other decreases, and
vice versa. Altruism is always a sacrifice in the sense that
what is given over to another is given up by the self. A gift
is a loss.

Contracts founder, then, on the ultimate sacrifice, the
giving up of one's life for one's friend. The purpose of all
contracts, all associations, is to balance the goods given and
received on both sides. Negotiations must, above all, be fair,
balanced equally on both sides. In such a view, self-sacrifice
is an absurdity, a giving up of the self that the contract was
meant to protect. To substitute for a hostage, to volunteer
to defend one's country in a war, to risk one's life to save
another from a fire or from drowning – all of these actions
go against the logic of contracts. In contractual thought,
self-sacrifice destroys the self as well as that self's fulfillment.
But altruism, instead of being balanced nicely with egoism,
swallows it up. Contractarians are often heroic, of course
– in battle as well as in other life-threatening crises. But
their heroism is different from that of communitarians. The
logic of their heroism is a calculus which plays the odds. A
contractarian who would risk his life for another must see
the odds as something less than 100% and hope that he will
escape. Otherwise, the rescue of his friend will be a tragedy
for him. In an egocentric contract, to will a 100% certain
renunciation of one's life for the sake of another would be a
form of masochistic madness.

Communities, however, thrive on self-sacrifice. For when
we identify others as our other selves, egoism and altruism are
not opposed. Rather, love of self and love of others coincide.
The good of those whom we identify as our other selves does
not compete with our own good, but, rather, constitutes it.
Thus, we do not need to negotiate and compromise, seeking a
balance between egoism and we do not need to negotiate and
compromise, seeking a balance between egoism and altruism.
For these vary directly. As one increases, so does the other.
What is given over to another is not given up for the self,
but rather cements a union between the two, as that one
single good belongs to both in common. A gift is not a loss,
but a gain. The ultimate sacrifice, then, does not contradict
community but is, rather, its high point. To substitute for a
hostage, to go to war to defend one's country, to give one's

life in the rescue of a stranger – all of these actions fit the logic of community perfectly. Self-sacrifice fulfills the self. There is no need to calculate the odds, to protect egoism from excessive altruism. For a self-seeking which is true to itself, finding its own fulfillment in taking another's good as its own, is entirely altruistic. Giving up one's life for a friend is not a masochistic madness, then, but the acquisition for oneself of the highest possible good: communion with the good of another. Such self-love is thoroughly altruistic, such altruism thoroughly self-fulfilling.

The logic of motivation, rooted in views of whether persons are solitary or relational, respectively, is inescapable, whatever the actual motives of individuals. Once we choose to view persons as detached individuals and then seek to construct artificial ties between them, the psychology of self-primacy makes those ties, not just artificial, but illusory. For the primacy of the detached individual requires an egocentric, ultimately murderous motivation which prevents the communion of one person's will with the good of another. On the other hand, if we choose to see individual persons not as detached atoms but as having a natural communality which allows us to identify each other as each other's other selves, then the altruistic motivation which generates community becomes possible. The primacy of communality requires an altruistic, ultimately self-sacrificing motivation which brings lover and beloved together in the mutual possession of a single good, the beloved's own. When a manager gives his life to save his salesman, he comes into a community that heals his ontological loneliness.

We have yet to examine this natural communality, which precedes altruistic love and is the real basis for identification and a shared good. Until this point of our analysis, the focus has been on motivation. Such a focus was meant to show how our psychology determines our ontology, how actions build or destroy community, depending on the motives of their agents. But we must turn now to that natural communality, to the ontology that is prior to altruism. Otherwise we would be left with the possibility that altruism itself is a snare and a delusion, and that the community that it seems to generate is as illusory as the results of egocentric contracts. We turn, then, to the communality that is prior to community, to individuals who are, in our original being, not atomic but relational.

CHAPTER IV

THE RANGE OF COMMUNITY

The men and women whom we admire for giving up their lives for their friends are either heroes or fools, then. The difference lies in their motives. One who dies for another out of altruistic love finds for himself an ontological fulfillment that far outweighs whatever other good he might have enjoyed if he had lived a longer life. But one whose relations with those he saves are contractual, so that he gives his life in a calculated effort to beat the odds, dies because of a tragic, perhaps even foolish, miscalculation. This conclusion is, to say the least, paradoxical. In order to see its complete logic, we need to explore some further questions that have to do with the range of community. Up until now, we have seen only how an act of altruistic love brings the lover into communion with some good of the beloved which the lover identifies as his own. That analysis has been enough to show the minimal requirement for community. For such altruism is the way to forge – indeed, the only way to forge – the tie that binds two into one without their ceasing to be two. But there is a totality implicit in any community, however brief and superficial it may seem.

One who says "Good morning" to his newsboy in a moment of altruistic love is, by love's relentless logic, implicitly laying down his life for him. One who disdains his newsboy in a moment of egocentric usage, on the other hand, is implicitly taking his newsboy's life away. Neither may think about the logic of his motives, nor explicitly intend its outcome. But the logic is there, nonetheless, and will become apparent in a crisis. Any moment of altruistic love is a moment in which one person puts his entire self at the service of the entire self of the one who is loved. Any moment of egocentric use or pleasure is a moment in which one person holds the other's whole self in bondage to his own entire set of needs. The range of community, then, is the entirety of each of the persons involved, not just one or two aspects in isolation from the whole person. To love someone at all is to love him wholly. To fail to love someone in any way whatsoever is to fail to love him at all.

But the range of community extends infinitely farther. For when any one person is bound to another in altruistic love, the lover forges a tie by which he is bound to all other persons as well, all persons of all time and all places. He

is, indeed, in communion not just with persons, but with
all other beings as well. Because the universe is just that –
a universe, not a pluriverse – there is a kind of totality to
community such that we are either in community with the
whole of being, or we are not in community at all. There is no
such thing as a small community which would include only
some people and not others, or only one part of the world
and not the rest. The range of community, as we shall see,
is the range of the universe itself. Community ranges over
all beings, of all times and places, as well. Nature is part of
community, too.

And yet – and here is another paradox about community – despite the totality of any community, a totality that
exists from the first moment of anyone's altruistic love for
anyone, community can nevertheless grow. It can increase
both extensively and intensively. My communion with a single friend, for example, though in some sense total from the
first moment of my love, can become deeper and broader,
richer and more fulfilling as time goes by. My friend's reciprocity can add to the depth of our communion. Our ongoing
associating with each other also makes our community more
real. And our communion, even though it somehow includes
all of humanity, and all of the rest of the community of being
as well, can, paradoxically extend its membership. With such
growth, of course, my ontological fulfillment, which in a very
real and important sense is total as soon as I begin to love,
can grow as well. A lifetime spent in loving is a lifetime of
ever-increasing ontological fulfillment. In some mysterious,
but explicable way, what is total can nevertheless increase.

In order to explore the range of community and the dynamics by which that range can be extended, we need an
understanding of the existential make-up of persons that is
more explicit than what we have already seen. We need,
moreover, an understanding of that wider reality, the universe, within whose boundaries we live and move and have
our being. We need an understanding of what unifies the
universe, and what unifies persons, so that the identification
of another as our other self is not just wishful thinking. The
detached individuals of social contract thought have no unity
prior to the contracts, which the contracts would ratify and
appropriate. Some such natural ties there must be, however,
lest altruistic love be as artificial, and community as illusory,
as are the external unities that contracts provide.

We can begin by posing and then solving the problem on
the psychological plane, where it is obvious to anyone with

some adult experience of human relationships. We are often cynical about the possibility of altruism on the part of human beings. Many people assume that human beings are innately selfish, and that it is naive and sentimental to expect anything else of ourselves and each other. A realistic view, so we fear, suspects others of wanting to use and manipulate us, and leads us to put up various defenses for our own protection. Experience teaches us, indeed, to exercise a double wariness: We must be careful of coming too close to anyone, lest our autonomy be swallowed up. But on the other hand, we must not stay too distant, lest we be lonely. The contractual solution soon seems attractive: we will "find spaces in our togetherness," negotiate compromises between closeness and autonomy, and thus have, if not the best of both worlds, at least some of the benefits of each.

As we have begun to see, however, community is a better solution, one which brings us into genuine communion and yet leaves our precious unique identities intact. But community requires negotiations, too, as well as compromises, *quid pro quo* exchanges, and cost-benefits analyses. But in a community, these are all motivated by the altruistic love which implies our willingness to die for each other. The negotiations, thus, are not due to some sort of opposition between self-love and love of another, between my good and that of my beloved. Rather, compromises become necessary, within a context of our total love for another, because of the finitude of human persons that we noted earlier. Each of us is limited in the length of time that we have to live, and in the fact that we live only one moment of our allotted time at a time, in succession with other moments. We are limited in the space that we can occupy, so that we cannot be in all places at once, even mentally – our mental processes occur in time and space, also. We are limited, too, in our physical strength and energy, and these are vulnerable to the weather, to aging and to other physical forces beyond our control. The central question, however, remains: What is the motivation by which we adjust to each other's physical limits? Our motives are either egocentric or altruistic. If the former, our negotiations will inhibit both our closeness and our autonomy, as we constantly strive to keep these two in balance. But if we are altruistic, then we will paradoxically find a greater fulfillment in adapting to our limitations than we might have found otherwise. And closeness and autonomy, as well as sacrifice and fulfillment, will coincide and even enhance each other.

This paradoxical solution to the problem of maintaining both closeness and autonomy becomes evident in a simple, ordinary example – a marriage between, say, a singer and a writer. Can two people with such different talents really identify with each other, each seeking the other's fulfillment as his own, and finding therein his own fulfillment as well? Must one sacrifice his career to the other? Can they find some sort of total communion, each one's whole self at one with the whole self of the other? Or must they go their separate ways in order to preserve their integrity as artists, their autonomy as persons?[24]

Common (i.e. contractual) wisdom would say that the writer must be wary of the contribution he makes to the singer's development as a singer, lest his own development as a writer suffer. The singer would be warned to be careful, too, for the same reason – in fostering her beloved's writing, she must take care for her own development as a singer. On the other hand, some concessions have to be made in the other direction. For if the writer gives complete priority to his writing, he will soon find himself alone. And the singer who always puts her singing first will soon be left to enjoy a solitary career. Even from the point of view of an enlightened altruism, there are pressures to compromise. The writer will wish his own development so as to have a self to offer for the singer's ontological healing, and the singer will wish her own development for a similar reason. Thus, there seem to be pressures from two directions, pressures to put some limits on love, on closeness, on community itself. And these pressures can easily become pressures to turn their community into a contract, with all of its murderous implications.

Another, deeper look at the psychology of altruism can solve this closeness-autonomy dilemma. The singer's identification with the writer takes the mere fact of the writer's existence as a writer as something good in its own right, as an absolute good or end. The singer thus says to the writer, at least implicitly, "I am willing to put my whole self, includ-

---

[24] The example is from Aquinas' treatise on love, *S. Th.* I-II, 27, 3, "Whether Similarity is a Cause of Love?" St. Thomas argues that some sort of similarity is absolutely necessary as a cause of love. He mentions the love between a singer and a writer in replying to Augustine's statement that a lover can love in his beloved that which he would not wish to be himself. St. Thomas replies that a singer and a writer do have a common ground: each possesses what he needs in order to succeed in his own art, even though their respective arts differ. Johann extends the argument to show that any two beings, no matter how dissimilar they are, have a common ground that enables them to identify with each other in love: the immanent presence of the One Creator. See *The Meaning of Love*, pp. 69-73.

ing my very identity as a singer, to the service of your full existence as the unique person that you are. I will thus give over to your writing career my time, my energy, my other resources, my very identity as the singer that I am. For your flourishing is my good, too." The singer, then, could find total ontological fulfillment in the sacrifice of her singing career to the writer's success as a writer. His success would be her fulfillment.

But of course, the writer's altruistic love for the singer leads him to make a similar offer, to give up his writing in favor of the singer's singing, in full confidence that, even though he sacrifices his fulfillment as a writer, he finds an alternative ontological fulfillment, in the support of his singer's singing, that is total. For her good is his good, too, thanks to his identification of it as his own. But in addition to these two possibilities, there is a whole range of options by which the two might combine careers, making various accommodations to each other's needs. In those options, neither will find the same professional development that he might have enjoyed as a single artist, but each does find an alternative ontological fulfillment that is as complete as any may be. A writer who writes less in order to support his beloved's singing may end up being less fulfilled as a writer than he might have been, but he is just as fulfilled as a person – indeed, perhaps more so. And a similar fulfillment, different but just as total, would come to a singer who sings less than she might have if she had not made concessions to her beloved's writing.

The point, then, is not how much we give up and what the other gives up in return. Giving and getting may be entirely one-sided, or they may be balanced off in various ways. The point is the motivation with which our agreements come about. When that is altruistic, then each not only says, "Your flourishing is my good, too," but also, "My flourishing is your good." Thus neither is masochistic, neither is sadistic. The two become one while yet remaining two. Both exist, and exist to the full. The inhibitions on their careers, or on any other kind of personal development that either might renounce in favor of the other, are not due to inhibitions on their love. Love is what must always be total, a total devotion to the other's welfare that bears an implicit self-sacrificing intent. Limits and inhibitions on such totality are due to the simple fact that none of us, finite beings that we are, can experience to the full each and every kind of fulfillment for which we have the capacity. None of us can lovingly support to the full each and every possible fulfillment that a beloved

has the capacity for. We must pick and choose. To go here
is to pass up going there, to develop this talent is to neglect
that, to speak this word of love is to omit many others that I
might have said, given infinite time and energy. Because time
and energy are finite, even as we are ourselves, community
calls for contracts as an element of its structure.

Closeness and autonomy, then, do not necessarily
threaten each other. If we understand them correctly, we
need not restrict one in order to protect the other. For to
love is, at one and the same time, to enhance the autonomy
of the beloved and, in so doing, to come close to it, to possess
it, even, as one's own. When we become friends, when we
enter community, we need to make many adjustments that
we would not have made if we had remained strangers. But
those adjustments are not due to any deficiencies in loving.
Loving is, and remains, total – a total gift of self, a total
support of the other's welfare, a total possession of, through
communion with, that welfare. The inhibitions we find, the
adjustments we make, the sacrifices by which we yield one
fulfillment in favor of another are due, rather, to the material limitations of a love that is human – bodily, temporal,
and located in space. Under the demands of love, then, a
writer has several options. He might maximize his writing
to the detriment of his beloved singer's singing. He might
sacrifice his writing entirely to her singing. Or he might do
some writing and sacrifice some. Circumstances can decide.
As long as he loves altruistically, his community with her,
and his ontological fulfillment, will be complete.

But there is another side of persons, too, the self-
transcendence which overcomes our finitude. That remarkable capacity for self-transcendence that we mentioned in an
earlier chapter is now worth another look. In our ability to
know, we transcend time and space, not only as these restrict
our own being, but in their restrictions of the being of our
beloved as well. And love, the love that identifies another's
self as my own, overcomes the beloved's "here-and-nowness"
in an even more powerful, more really effective, way. I can
know a beloved as both here and there, both now and then.
And in a single moment of altruistic love, I can come into
possession not only of what my beloved is here and now, but
also of what he has been, will be, might have been, could
yet be, there and then. His total existence as a person, past,
present, and future, actual and possible, becomes my possession in a moment. Thus the range of our community is total,
the entire being of the one loved.

Let us look again at our singer-writer couple. The singer, as a singer, is, of course, much more than that. She is a woman of a certain shape and size. She has other talents. She has physical strength and beauty, a state of health, a set of family relationships, her thought processes, values, decisions and choices. She has her basic human nature, her citizenship, and so on. All of these traits have a history and a possible future. She has, moreover, her love for her writer and her acceptance of his love for her. But she is not just a bundle of traits, these and others too numerous to mention, too changeable to grasp, too complex to organize in such a way that all may be explicitly loved. Fundamental to her make-up, even as that shifts and changes over time, is the actuality that unifies and stabilizes all her traits – her existential act, her being. It is by that existential actuality that she is a really existent person, rather than a mere possibility. And it is by that existential actuality that all of her components are unified into a single subsistent entity – the entity that we designate by her name. Thanks to that unifying existential act, she has a stable, unified and recognizable identity as the unique person that she is.

This existential unity is crucial to any love that would be real rather than abstract. If we look at our singer's various qualities sex, eye color, singing talent, and so on – we see that each of them is communicable. That is, many persons might also be female, blue-eyed, endowed with singing talent, and so on. Abstraction, by which we mentally isolate some one aspect of a person from that person's other aspects, automatically leads us to what is common to that individual and an infinite number of other individuals, either actual or possible. And, as we have seen, a decision to love someone on the basis of such an abstraction leads only to a contractual association, a friendship of utility or pleasure. Such love is partial, not total. Such associations are necessarily abstract, depersonalizing, egocentric, ultimately murderous and anticommunal. The only basis for a genuine communion between two persons is a love directed toward the concrete totality of that person. In such love, the unique, individual, total reality of that person is taken as a good in its own right.

Such love, then, the altruism which identifies the beloved's entire existential good as the lover's own, must be directed toward the unified, concrete totality of that person. In other words, to love someone is, fundamentally to affirm that person's existential act as a good in its own right. It follows that such love cannot be selective. An altruistic lover

says, "I love you for who you are – for all of who you are,
who you have been, who you will be, who you might have
been and are not and never will be." In loving someone's
existential act, we love all that the act actualizes, all of that
person's concrete reality, for its own sake. In the words of
the old song, "Most of all, I love you 'cause you're you." Any
love short of that would be abstract, thus partial, contractual, and egocentric. But love that is concrete, that is an
affirmation of the beloved's very existence, is by that very
fact an affirmation of the entire reality of the one who is
loved. And by that affirmation, the lover joins to himself,
in real community, the beloved's entire self – not just what
is real here and now, but the beloved's total existence, past
and future as well as present. The range of community is
thus total as regards its extension within the self of the one
who is loved.

It follows that such love – the only tie that binds – is
unconditional as well. For the singer's existence is absolutely
fundamental. It is not just her most important feature. It is
the actuality by which all her other traits, her very identity
as the individual person that she is, are real. Remove her
existence, and she cannot sing, does not have blue eyes, is
not a woman – in short, she doesn't exist. But support her
existence, affirm it in love, and you affirm the rest as well.
Bind yourself, with the ties of love, to someone's existence,
and you are bound to the whole of that person. Such love
can only be unconditional. For if our writer were to put
conditions on his love – I will love you only as long as you
are healthy, or famous, or fun to be with, or supportive to
my writing – his love would be instantly transformed into an
egocentric contract. And then community would be instantly
and totally lost.

Love, then, if it is to generate real community instead
of an egocentric contract, cannot be selective or conditional,
looking to only part of the beloved's self. For to affirm only
part of the beloved's reality – the part that meets one's conditions – is to focus love on a part abstracted from the whole.
Such an abstract focus immediately makes the beloved's good
relative to something in me, a means to my ends, and thus
the object of an egocentric search for my own fulfillment. In
the final analysis, then, anyone's love for anyone else, if it is
to be communal, must be what our marriage vows say: "for
better, for worse, for richer, for poorer, in sickness and in
health, until death do us part." If our writer does marry his
singer with such love in his heart, he could conceivably find

that all their thoughts about concessions for meshing two careers go out the window one fine day when his wife is injured or made an invalid by some severe illness. He may then give up his writing in order to care for her, with a devotion that consumes the rest of their years together. Singing and writing both go down the drain. Such devotion will make perfect sense, though, in light of his original affirmation of her existence. And the change in his life plans will not detract in the least from his own fulfillment as a person. For that fulfillment does not lie in his writing career, nor in her singing. It is found in community. Community might mean sharing in her singing, or sharing with her his own writing. But it may just as well mean the sacrifice of both of these. He is healed ontologically by his communion with her whole person, whatever that wholeness may, over the course of years, turn out to be.

Love that is conditional, partial, abstractive would justify a divorce in the circumstances just described. Once the wife became an invalid, her husband might say, "Sorry, this isn't what I bargained for." Exactly. Selective, abstractive, conditional love is precisely a bargaining process. To say that communal love must be unconditional – and thus permanent and faithful – is not to say, of course, that everyone must marry everyone whom they love. It is also not to say that we are excused from loving everyone except the one to whom we are married. But we do mean to say that the very nature of love is such that, if it is to be communal rather than contractual, it must be total, unconditional, and permanent in some way that is closely comparable to the mutual devotion of spouses. But within this context of total devotion, many limits will have to be negotiated – limits on the possible partial ways of acting out the totality of love.

To take an obvious example, I don't give the same attention, time, energy, money and other resources to a business colleague that I give to my spouse. But the limits that I place on my business associations must be based on what is appropriate to various roles and relationships, what is dictated by circumstances. They must not be due to any limits on my loving devotion to my colleagues. I must not have a love for them that is conditional, temporary, selective or in any way restricted by egocentric motivation. Such relations would be contractual, and thus anti-communal and ultimately murderous. Restrictions that are based on what is appropriate to various roles, relations and circumstances do not inhibit the totality of community. That is, when I miss

an important business meeting in order to be at home with
my sick spouse, I am not loving my spouse more than I love
my business colleagues. For I love both, all, totally – with
my whole self at the service of their every need. I give my
time and attention to one instead of another because of the
rules, roles, and relations which structure our loving associations. In other circumstances, I might leave a sick spouse
to his own devices in order to meet with my colleagues – but
not because I then love my colleagues more. Always, I love
everyone totally, equally, affirming their existence as a good
in its own right. But the actions by which I carry out that
devotion will vary according to rules, roles, and relations.
What counts is my unflagging altruism. But any action, any
omission, any inward attitude, even that of a moment, that is
rooted in egocentric motives destroys community at its base.

Given that every community is total, then, in its first
moment of reciprocal altruism, how can community grow,
deepen, extend itself? How can that which is already total
reach a greater range? Only one mode of growth is possible:
what is implicit must become explicit. Here, we see a difference between the way we transcend ourselves in cognition and
the way we do so in love. Love, true, is rooted in knowledge:
in one way, we cannot love what we do not know. Without
knowledge of a good, and of someone to whom we might wish
it, we cannot wish that good to anyone, ourselves or another.
But in another way, we can love what we do not know. We
can love more than we know. And in so doing, we love implicitly what we do not explicitly know. Love, in its beginning,
is total – an affirmation of the entire existential perfection
of the beloved. Such love has to be based on a knowledge
that is sufficient for the lover to identify the beloved whose
existence he wants to affirm. Our writer, if he is to love our
singer, must at least know who she is. But such knowledge
can be quite minimal in its explicit content. The love that
is always total, then – as a devotion to her very existence –
grows as its content becomes more and more explicit.

Suppose our singer loves her writer with a similar total
devotion, with this same willingness to affirm his total reality
as the unique person that he is. She says, in effect, "I love
you. For your sake, I want you to be all that you can be, and I
am putting my whole self at the service of your whole being."
She does not yet know, in explicit detail, what constitutes the
"all" that he can be. She knows little of what he has been in
the past, of events which still condition what he is now. She
knows, apart from conjecture, nothing of what he will be in

the future. And yet, she can love the past and future that she does not know. As our words *promise* and *commitment* show (both are derived from Latin roots meaning "to send forward"), she can, indeed, must put her very self at the ready to support the self that her lover becomes and reveals as time goes by.

The growth of her love, then, consists in coming to love explicitly what she has already loved implicitly. As their community brings them into closer associations with each other, she sees more and more clearly what her writer's needs are, and moves to supply them as best she can. She also sees, in ever more explicit detail, what his good is, the unique personal good, that she can simply enjoy as her own because she has wedded herself to it. Thus, it is quite one thing for her to say, at the beginning of their romance, "I want what is best for you," and to say later on, when she knows more, "I want you to know this bit about my past so that you can laugh about it along with me." Likewise, it is quite one thing to say, early in a marriage, "I'm all yours – ask me anything you want," when we love more than we know. But it is quite another thing to say, later on, when we know more, "I've ordered tickets for your favorite play, which was just announced this morning. I knew you'd want to go." The implicit has become explicit, and love has grown accordingly.

In a sense, then, later love – love based on long familiarity – is no greater in its range than is beginning love. For love was total in its first moment. First love, expressing a global, largely implicit concern, instantly generates a communion that is total, encompassing the whole selves of both lover and beloved. And yet that later love, more explicit, more precise, and more detailed, is greater. Love grows as we pass from loving more than we know, to knowing what we have already loved, and then loving it anew. As love grows, we extend the range of community. We reach love's high point when we become familiar with as much of a beloved as we can, through years of rapt attention. It is then that we can speak the word which, alone among all words, expresses the whole of the unique personal identity of a beloved: his name. In English usage, we capitalize names. They are proper nouns, special to persons in their unique individual wholeness. We do not capitalize the common nouns that refer to various qualities abstracted from the wholeness: blue-eyed, a male, a writer. But a person's name refers to his self, his whole self, and nothing but his self. There is a communal wisdom in this simple rule of grammar, which requires us to capitalize our names as proper nouns. For they name our existential act, and all the rest of the concrete self that the existential act makes real.

Further analysis shows, though, that even the so-called common, abstractable qualities of people are not really common at all, except in our minds. In the real world, a salesman's skills are his and his alone. He cannot communicate them to anyone else. He might develop similar skills in another, but then, that person's skills would be his, not those of his mentor. The same is true for any other feature of a person. Humanity is not really common to all of us, but unique in each of us, and thus multiple in the world. I can no more confer my humanity on someone else than I can my cooking, teaching, or singing skills, my green eyes, my square knuckles, or my memories. Human nature is individualized in a unique way in each of us, and is thus incommunicable. Even existence, seemingly the most common feature of all, extending beyond humans to all beings of all kinds, is not really common at all. If my existence could belong to anyone else, that person would be me, and I would be he. Existence is uniquely individualized, even as we are ourselves. It becomes common to two only in love, when a lover chooses to make a beloved's existence his own.

These points take us beyond a psychological analysis of community and of the love that produces it. They take us into the realm of metaphysics, where we now must look at the prerequisites of altruistic love, especially of the identification that is its heart and soul. If I am to identify with another as my other self, there must be some real basis for this mental act, some existential communality between us. Otherwise my identification, having no basis in reality, will produce only an illusion of community. In order to merely associate with another, I must see some likeness between us, some way in which to make him similar to myself. Contracts are based on a supply and demand relation between lover and loved. The lover has a need, and the beloved has precisely what will fulfill that need. Emptiness calls to fullness as the egocentric person seeks what is useful and/or pleasant to himself.

But a question remains about the very possibility, the metaphysical possibility, of friendships of the third kind. That question, completely fundamental, is about the ontological conditions that must obtain if the act of identification is to be authentic. When someone does identify another as his other self, with whom he will possess a single good in common, is he indulging in wishful thinking? When I seek to make another person my other self, what is there about the two of us that allows such identification to be real rather than a fantasy? Identification is a psychological process that has ontological consequences: the generation of community. In order for us to have those ontological consequences, there must also be some prior ontological conditions. What kind of links between two entirely, existentially unique and diverse individuals can make it possible for them to become, not just like each other, but one with each other? Without some such ontological tie, the tie that binds us to each other in community is mere wishful thinking. Community, then, would fall by the wayside, and contracts, with their ultimately murderous intent, would be the only human associations with any basis in reality. And yet, the existence of another, which love bids me identify as my own, is precisely incommunicable. It can belong to no one else. Furthermore, since it actualizes, realizes, the other's entire being, the other seems, precisely as a concrete whole, incommunicable. It seems that I cannot really possess, be in communication with, my beloved other at all – not in his totality, and not in any of his parts.

The question is, in the final analysis, whether existence itself is common or diverse, one or many, or some combination of these. If it is entirely diverse, totally different from one being to another, then all of our perceptions of reality are questionable. For if existence is, in any one case, "that which renders something an actual being instead of a mere possibility," then in all other cases it would have to be something else. And then all other things would have to be something other than actual beings. No community would be possible, then, for what is an actual being can in no way be one with what is not an actual being. On the other hand, if what makes one entity be an actual being is also what makes another be an actual being, so that existence is entirely the same in the two cases, the two are not two beings, but one. The husband in *United States* who said, "Please, Libby, only one of us can be me" stated half of the dilemma. But he left the other horn in place: if only one of us can be me, then you can't, and neither can anyone else. There is no way in which we can be existentially united. Community is never a reality, then, but only a fiction.

There are ways, though, to escape between the horns of this dilemma of the one and the many. One escape makes all of reality a single being, of which all of us are parts or appearances. In that view, community is not real because its members do not exist. Only the supra-mundane one is real.

Another escape makes us so diverse that we can never have anything in common. And then community cannot be real because we are radically, and always, many, never unified except in our wishful thoughts. But there is a third way, a view of reality in which beings, while diverse in themselves, even in their very existence, are unified by their common relation to a single transcendent being that is their common source, their common goal, and their common exemplar. Thus they share common relationships to some transcendent One, and those common relations can be the basis for the act of identification. When we identify with another person, then, making him our other self, we are appropriating, in mind and will, a unity that is already the case. We both proceed, in our diverse ways, from a common source. We do not merge into a single reality, but share, in love, a common connection to a transcendent One that we already share ontologically.[25]

In this third view, likeness and difference, community and diversity are not opposed to each other but in some sense require each other. Paradoxically, only similar beings can be different – for in order to differ, they must exist, and thus be similar in that fundamental actuality. And yet, only different beings can be similar to each other. For in order to be similar, they must be many, and thus differ somehow, each having something that the other lacks. A single being cannot be similar to itself. And to complete the paradox, that by which these similar beings differ is precisely that by which these different beings are similar: the act of existence by which each one is but one actually existing entity out of a multitude of actually existing entities. Some of our proverbs about community – pithy sayings which, after all, do have some basis in common experience – express this metaphysical paradox. On the one hand, "Opposites attract." But on the other hand, "Birds of a feather flock together." Couples are encouraged to find what they have in common. But on the other hand, marriages break up because the spouses are "just too much alike." The reality of community depends, finally, on this paradoxical relationship of the one and the many.

The problem is most acute where it is most concrete – in love's demand for self-sacrifice. For the logic of the action by which I identify someone other than myself as my other self is puzzling, indeed. How can what is other than myself

---

[25] See Johann's account of the community of being at pp. 76-80 of *The Meaning of Love.*

be myself? The "otherness" is completely radical: I have my own act of being, utterly unique, completely individualized as mine, and thus incommunicable. My being cannot be exchanged for that of anyone else. My being cannot be shared with anyone else. And my would-be beloved's being is equally unique, individualized, incommunicable – his alone. The "manyness" of being is not to be denied.

Such radical incommunicability seems to make community impossible. My effort to make another self my other self seems but wishful thinking – to make his being my being can only be play-acting or self-delusion. Moreover, the self- sacrifice that is implicit in any identification becomes the height of folly. How can I logically subordinate my welfare to the welfare of someone who is radically, ineluctably alien to me? How, in other words, prefer his good to mine when the two are incomparable? The question arises whether our exchange is trivial or profound. Why, for example, should I deny myself a movie in order to give a small Christmas bonus to my newsboy? He is a separate, alien being, whose well being can never be mine, no matter how much I might wish or pretend that it is. In graver matters, why should I die in order to save someone else? A missed movie might bring some compensation – a warm glow of Christmas cheer in my own heart as I enjoy my newsboy's enjoyment, say. But where's my gain, my self-fulfillment, in rescuing a drowning baby at the cost of my own life? In neither case, it seems, do I add any being to my own. But in giving up my life, I seem to suffer complete and utter loss. And yet, the altruistic love which generates community makes such complete sacrifice an implicit part of its own intrinsic logic.

We are faced, then, with a metaphysical puzzle, one which requires a metaphysical solution. Granted the radical manyness of persons (as of all other beings of our experience), we must find some transcendent unity among them. If my beloved's being, and thus his entire make-up, is radically incommunicable, radically his own and not mine, we can only come together as one if we share a common relationship to some one Being that is transcendent to us both. A creationist metaphysics takes that transcendent One, the ground of the many, to be God. This view of reality allows us to admit the full individuality, thus diversity, of persons and yet find a unity among them that makes identification possible. In this world view, all the beings of the finite world receive, by an ongoing activity of a Creator, their uniquely diversified acts of existence. That ongoing creative activity is the presence within all beings of a Creator who is an infinitely perfect being, purely actual, not restricted by time and space, by individuality, or by any specific nature. The world, then, including the race of men and more, is itself a community, the community of being. The ultimate units of the world are not detached, atomic monads, but a multitude of diverse beings that form an ordered network because of the shared presence within them of their Creator. That Creator, however, is perfectly One and in no sense many. He has no multiplicity within Him, of parts or aspects that are distinct from each other. He is utterly Simple and Indivisible. His being, then, is not dispersed in time and space as ours is. Rather, it is Eternal and Omnipresent. Thus, the Creator is not partly present here and partly there, but totally present here and there, and everywhere else. His existence is not a succession of moments, with a past now lost and a future yet to come, but is now, all at once. His entire existence, then, infinite in its perfection, is present in each and every one of us at each and every moment of our lives.

The Creator, thus, is both completely transcendent to the world and totally immanent in it. The existence that He supplies to each being is truly its own, not His nor that of any other being. The diverse existential acts are truly incommunicable. And yet, each such act of existence is rooted in, and constantly derived from, the same Source as is every other such act of existence. The world is a universe – not a single being, and not a disorganized multitude, but an ordered, unified multitude. It is the community of being, in which many beings are made one without ceasing to be many. In such a world, human love, when it is altruistically motivated, is but the appropriation, in conscious choice, of a community that is already the case. To love is to affirm, in a conscious and free act, the unity that already obtains between lover and beloved – their common membership in the community of being. The human members of any community are not detached atoms whose ties to each other are artificially constructed by their own wishful thinking, or their defensive egoism. Instead, our altruistic love constitutes a psychological tie that reduplicates the ontological tie that binds us together even before we begin to love. The tie that already binds, moreover, the Creator's presence, does not just unify all persons, but all beings of nature as well.

When I love someone, then, with the kind of love that generates community, what I basically do is to wish to him the place in the community of being that is already his. True,

I identify his good as my own, and that good is his fully flourishing existence as the unique individual that he is. But my respect for his existence, which leaves his individuality intact even as I identify it as my good, has implications that reach out to the rest of the universe. For in wishing my friend his fully flourishing existence as the unique individual that he is, I implicitly wish for all the conditions that are necessary for that flourishing. It would be poor love, for example, that would say, "Well, yes, I want you to succeed as a writer, but I don't care whether or not you have enough to eat." Having enough to eat is a condition for his success as a writer. But the most important condition for his success as a writer is the presence in him of his Creator. Without that presence, his existence is lost, and with it everything else besides, including his success as a writer.

This metaphysics of love, by which altruism is, most fundamentally, the affirmation of the beloved's membership in the community of being, has profound implications for the range of community. We have already seen how any love that is altruistic is also total, unconditional, permanently faithful, centered on the whole of the beloved's personal self. The range of community, with regard to the ontological make-up of a single beloved, is total. Community includes his entire self. But now we can see how the love of any one person extends beyond that person to include others as well – all who enjoy membership in the community of being. In fact, we now can see a further logic to love, such that to love one person is to love all, including oneself, and to fail to love any person is to fail to love all, including oneself. The range of community, in fact, is not even restricted to persons, since all beings, of all kinds and levels, make up the community of being. All exist by the creative indwelling of the one God. There is, then, an ultimate logic to love, by which to love any single being – a slug, or a rock – is to love all. And to fail to love any single being – a slug, or a rock – is to fail to love all, including oneself.

That logic begins with the community of being as its premise. All the beings of the created universe, those of all times and all places, form a network. They are unified by the presence within them of the Creator, Who is Simple, Eternal and Omnipresent. His presence is indivisible, total and complete in each unit of space and of time, in each being. Thus when I wish to anyone his membership in the community of being, and all the conditions on which that membership depends, I wish to him the ongoing total presence within him of

the Creator. Since that presence is indivisible, I cannot logically wish it to one person and not to another, for it cannot
be so divided and restricted. Thus in wishing the presence
of the Creator to any one person, I implicitly wish it to all
others as well. That presence cannot be parceled out, and
so, I must wish it everywhere or not wish it at all. In wishing
that presence to all, I wish the totality of all those beings.
For that totality is the constant effect of the presence of the
Creator. When I affirm any single being, then – it need not
even be a person – I affirm them all, the entire community
of being. To love one is to love all. And to fail to love one is
to fail to love all.

That one whom I love – or fail to love – could well be
myself. The way in which altruism and self-love finally coincide in a metaphysics of community is now evident. Aristotle
had observed that a friend of the third kind, who loves others
for their sakes rather than his own, is, by that very fact, his
own best friend as well. The Greek philosopher was more
right than he knew. For in our altruistic loving, we wish for
ourselves the greatest good that can possibly be wished to
anyone: our own full appropriation of the entire community
of being. That appropriation brings a total ontological healing, a communion with all beings, of all times and places.
Thus, our need to exist beyond the limits of our own finitude
is satisfied as completely as it can be. True, we find this
healing only in wishing it to others for their sakes, but in a
paradoxical way, we can wish it for ourselves for our sakes,
too. And we can do so in a way that is not egocentric. For
once we understand the paradox that self-fulfillment comes
only through devotion to the fulfillment of others, the very
moment that we begin to desire our own fulfillment, we can
move at once into the altruism that is our only path to it.
An enlightened self-seeking becomes an altruism without re-
serve. And then the communion with being that is our own
fulfillment is immediately put at the service of those whom
we love.

In wishing such fulfillment for ourselves, however, we do
not seek it directly or make it our motive for associating
with other people. Rather, the self-seeking that is the root
of all our actions becomes at once our best effort at self-
forgetfulness, at self-abandon, at self-sacrifice and devotion.
Our motivation becomes a generosity that knows no bounds,
because it searches out the entire range of community. And
that range, the community of being, is the entire universe.
Any act of altruistic love – no matter how seemingly triv-

ial, how brief, how hidden – is an appropriation of the entire community of being. Any act of such love is thus a total healing of a lover's ontological loneliness. By the logic of love, to possess, through identification, any good of any being is to possess, at least implicitly, the total good of every being in the universe. Any altruistic lover, in any of his acts, transcends himself as completely as any creature might do. He overcomes his being "only human, only myself, only here, only now." For in his loving communion with the entire community of being, he also loves, and thus communes with, the Creator Who is the source of it all. He thus possesses as his own the infinity of perfectly actual being, eternal and omnipresent.

The range of our fundamental community thus has no bounds – no boundaries in time or space, no restrictive clauses limiting its membership to some beings and not others. Questions about the size of various communities within the community of being are, of course, important. So are those of geographic location, temporal limits, material resources that make up budgets, qualifications of those who partake in a community's activities, and so on. But these concerns – the concerns of sociologists, political theorists, family planners and so on – have to do not with the nature of community, but with the practicalities of acting out the basic reality of community as it exists in the hearts of the lovers who are its members. For any other community, any smaller community contained within the community of being – a family, a city, a professional association, a nation – is a grouping of only some of the persons that make up the entire human community. The entire human community (indeed, the entire community of being) is, in the final analysis, the only community that there is. That community is what exists prior to anyone's loving, and that community is what is appropriated in its entirety whenever anyone loves anyone altruistically. The only real community, then, includes everyone and everything, and extends to all times and places. That community exists in the mind and heart of each person who loves.

There is, then, a second totality to community, a totality that happens from the first moment of community's reality in any loving heart. And yet, like the totality that we saw growing in a one-to-one relationship in a marriage or a friendship, this larger totality can grow, too. And it grows in exactly the same way – by our making explicit what is only implicit in community's first moment. Just as I love the totality of a

spouse or friend from the first moment of affirming his existence, so do I love the totality of the community of being in
the first moment of affirming the existence of any being. But
just as my love for, and communion with, my friend grows as
we associate with each other, so does my communion with all
of being. I love that entire community implicitly whenever I
love anything or anyone at all. In so doing, I love much more
than I know. But I grow to love more explicitly as I know
more explicitly. Here, then, is the place of smaller human
"communities" within the overall community of being, and
even of nature and her various kingdoms.

Families, nations and other "smaller communities" are,
in effect, devices by which we who are already in community
by our altruistic love associate with each other in order to
make that love more explicit in its details, and in its outward
expression. These are ways by which we focus our attention
more directly on some persons, but within a continuing global
concern for all. They are devices by which we, who cannot be
present to all in time and space, become present to, and familiar with, some people in some times and some places. But
again, that familiarity does not detract from the fundamental
love for all which alone can make community real. True, I love
my family "more" than I love strangers, and my countrymen
"more" than those of foreign lands. Love becomes greater as
familiarity does. I set priorities in the time, money, energy
that I expend toward those I love. When I have to choose,
my time and attention go to my spouse before a friend, to my
children before other children, to my colleagues before those
to whom I have no professional ties. Love is greater, more
extensive and more intensive, toward some members of the
community of being than toward others. It is more explicit
and more precise in its details.

And yet, this growth of community, as love becomes more
explicit within smaller circles of familiarity, cannot detract
from the original totality by which in loving any one being
we love all. There are limits, in other words, to how I may
set my priorities and preferences, so that I always owe to every single person, even strangers, the self-sacrificing devotion
that is implicit in any moment of altruistic love. To love anyone is to be willing to give up my life for him. And to love
anyone is to love everyone. This fundamental totality of love
is, in fact, not far from our common experience. Aristotle noticed that we give directions to strangers when they ask, and
help them up when they fall – "As if every man were naturally a friend to every man." When we look at that friendship

for strangers in the context of a creationist metaphysics, we see that we owe our lives to everyone, given certain circumstances, because to love one is to love all. A simple example makes this totality clear: if I am walking down the street and see a stranger's child toddling into traffic, communal impulses would send me into the street to save him, even at the sacrifice of my own life. The logic of altruistic love – unlike the logic of contracts – would not allow me to stand there and watch, thinking, "Gee, isn't that too bad? I'm glad it isn't one of my children."

From the moment when we first begin to love, then, the totality of the community of being is ours. Our love extends to all, with a self-sacrificing devotion. But that total devotion grows as, through various communal associations, we come to know in ever more explicit detail what that devotion really means, concretely, in regard to some selected persons. Those special ones, the ones we love more explicitly, are our family members, our countrymen, and others who become our familiars in our various associations. But in a communal world, all communal associations are fundamentally different from those that are based on contracts. For contracts are exclusive. Contractual love is given only to the parties to the contract, and not to others. Our terms of endearment, spoken only to a select few, express the terms of our endearment. They are ways in which we give conditional love to certain selected people, in certain times and places. Such contracts bring us no communal healing at all. But it is different in community: one who loves some more than others within the community of being forms associations that do not detract from, but rather extend and intensify, his basic loving devotion to all beings of all times and places. Communal associations intensify and extend our ontological healing, by making explicit what is implicitly complete from its first moment – our appropriation of the community of being, in altruistic love.[26]

---

[26] Glenn Tinder makes a fine differentiation of a community from a society in *Community, Reflections on a Tragic Ideal*, pp. 105-113. The distinction is the theme of the chapter, which is entitled, "Paradoxical Patriotism."

CHAPTER V

COMMUNITY AND HUMANISM

A metaphysics which sees all of being as a community, a community which we appropriate in altruistic love, obviously accords well with the beliefs of the world's great Biblical religions. Moslems, Christians, Jews – all believe in God as Creator of the world, and all prescribe love of neighbor as one of the great commandments that govern the moral lives of their believers. All honor martyrdom and self-sacrifice as the height of such love. In the light of such a metaphysics, we can see why the great saints of these religions considered themselves to be, not saints, but sinners. A saint is one who loves well, with that steady generosity that we have been calling altruistic love. And yet, all of the recognized saints of Judaism, Islam and Christianity have considered themselves to be failures precisely in love of God and of neighbor. These holy people, clearly, were not putting on a false humility. Neither were they degrading themselves in a sort of unhealthy masochism. They simply realized more vividly than the rest of us the implications of love, and thus the implications of love's failures.

The saints took what we would consider to be minor failures – say, a moment's indifference to a stranger, a failure to offer a cup of water – as very serious failures, indeed. For they knew that any failure in loving anybody is a failure to love everybody. When I deny my love to anyone, even a stranger, I implicitly deny it to everyone else, too, no matter how I might rationalize. Any denial of love is a refusal of the entire community of being, a rejection of God wherever He is found. Any small act of selfishness, even of indifference, utterly destroys community. For the failure to love a stranger is not just a failure to love that person at that moment. It is a failure to love the entire community of being, including myself. If total community, an appropriation of the entire community of being, is a possibility of every moment, then every moment is precious indeed. Every missed opportunity for loving is a missed opportunity for community, for the total community that heals our ontological loneliness completely. Each failure to love thus radically reinforces our ontological loneliness, even as each moment of love brings its complete healing. Either I appropriate all of being, or none of it.

We are driven with the saints, then – driven by the logic of love itself – to look to our motives. Those motives are

87

obviously egocentric when we refuse love outright, when we use, manipulate or hurt another person. But – as the saints realized so well – they are also egocentric when we simply fail to love when we could have. Indifference carries the same murderous implications that egocentric associations imply. But there is still another deeper implication to love's logic, once love is set in the context of the community of being. I must question my motives, not only when I utterly fail to love, but also when I attempt to love in a selective fashion. When I love some aspects of a friend but not others, when I love some people but not others, then I must ask myself why I love what I do love. My reasons for loving the people that I choose to love, the people that I prefer over others, must be suspect. My reasons for loving any one person selectively, conditionally, must be suspect, too. When the love of one person – a total, self-sacrificing devotion that I purport to have for one person –excludes a similar devotion to any and all others, then I must ask why I love the ones I do love. And the reason will inevitably be that I love them for the sake of some use or pleasure that I find in them for myself. In other words, selective love is inevitably egocentric, and thus anti-communal. When I love some people but not others, I obviously fail to come into community with the ones that I do not even claim to love. But my failure is even more profound: I also fail to come into community with those whom I purport to love. When I love only those who are good for me in some way, I love them as related to me, not as other selves. Thus, it is myself that I love primarily, not them. Such self-primacy precludes my community with anyone and everyone. It is, indeed, a refusal of my own fully flourishing existence as a member of the community of being. And so, selective love of others fails even as love of self. For genuine love of self is love of self as integrated into the community of being.

When I love selectively, then, I seek to parcel out what cannot be parceled out: the omnipresence of the Creator. Since His creative act is all of a piece, I cannot wish it to some and not to others. I must wish it for all, including myself, if I will it to anyone. Moreover, I cannot wish it to an individual on some terms and not others. I must love totally or not at all. The egocentric individual who is the subject of contractual associations, by the same logic, lacks the love of self by which his own existence might flourish. We can see, then, in the light of such failures to appropriate the community of being, how profoundly an egocentric individual defeats his own ontological healing. His indeed is the profound masochism, the truly metaphysical self-contempt. The saint, on the other hand, who berates himself for seemingly trivial failures in loving, wishes for himself his own proper good: his full participation in the community of being. His is the true self-love, the metaphysical self-esteem that coincides with humility. The Biblical "Love thy neighbor as thyself" – not "more than thyself," not "instead of thyself," not "as if he were thyself," but precisely "as thyself" – accords perfectly with a metaphysics of being that takes the world to be unified by the omnipresence of its Creator.

But now another question arises: we must wonder whether community is necessarily linked to a Biblical religious faith. Is a creationist metaphysics necessary as a philosophical premise? The argument offered so far allows utterly diverse persons to unite, without detriment to their precious individuality. Their communion is but their appropriation, in conscious choice, of each other's membership in a community of being. How important is this premise? Is community possible for non-believers and philosophical atheists? Is community possible in "a world come of age," in which we humans have won our freedom from the deity? Is community dead to those for whom God is dead? Can humanists generate true community, with all its implications of self-sacrificing devotion, unconditional and faithful love, ontological healing? Are contracts, with their murderous as well as masochistic implications, the only hope for those who do not believe that "In the beginning, God created heaven and earth"? What are we to make of the undeniable fact that many atheists, many secular humanists, are more honest and kind, more sensitive and generous, more ardent for justice and world peace, than are many of the "People of the Book"? What, exactly, is the relation between community and religion, community and humanism?

The humanism of our contemporary society began, after all, as a reaction against the superstitions and fears, the violations of human freedom and dignity, the denial of human rights, the wars, even, that were perpetrated in the name of organized religion. What should have been community par excellence turned out instead to be a spirit of contempt for human life in this world. In looking to the next life, many believers easily tolerated anti-communal attitudes and institutions which still plague us: racism, sexism, exploitation of the poor by the rich and of the weak by the strong. In a world deeply influenced by the Enlightenment, a humanism which treasures persons just for being persons here and now, seeking equal dignity, equal rights and equal freedom for all, seems seductive indeed. Religious believers have shown us all too clearly how loving God in our neighbor, and loving our neighbor in God, can easily turn out to be ways of not loving our neighbor at all. At first glance, an atheistic human-ism would seem to be an impossible approach to community. Without some sort of entity that is transcendent to all per-sons and yet resident in each one, there would seem to be no basis for the identification that is required for altruistic love. For if two are to come together as one, there must be some common basis, some pre-existing unity between them which the lover can appropriate. Without a transcendent source of unity, two human persons are totally diverse, totally alien from each other. In that case, their communality has to be artificially constructed. They can come together because of needs and talents that mesh with one another. But in that case their friendship would be one of utility. They can come together because of common interests and projects and goals. But in that case, their friendship is one of pleasure. One per-son might identify another as his other self, thus loving him altruistically, on the basis of a common humanity, a com-mon citizenship, a common racial or sexual identity. But all of these communalities are abstractions, generating only ab-stract, and thus unreal, unities. Humanism seems to leave us with the problem we noted earlier: to love someone in his full, concrete individuality – which is to say, as the person that he really is – is to love him as someone utterly diverse from myself. And if I am to respect that diversity, I cannot identify him as my other self. The "other" is so extreme that it overcomes the "my." It is this consideration which led us to a creationist metaphysics in the first place.

Our options are not quite so stark as they may seem, however. If we look more carefully at humanism, and draw out some of its implications, we can see how community might be possible for those who have no religious beliefs, or no explicit adherence to the creationist metaphysics outlined above. In this examination of humanism, we will be driven to state the absolute minimum, rock bottom requirement for the realization of community. That requirement is, in a word, sincerity.[27] The implications of sincerity, paradoxically, will

---

[27] This phenomenology of sincerity is adapted from Edward L. Rousseau's "Dia-logue and the Atheist," in *Continuum* 3, 3, Autumn 1965, pp. 398-399, and further developed in my own "Problems of Dialog: Invincible Ignorance"(*Listening*, 5, Winter, 1970) pp. 67-71.

allow for the possibility of any sincere person's being a communal person. They will, in fact, enable atheistic humanists to be more communal than many self-styled metaphysicians and believers. As we can now see, at a deeper level, the entity known as community is a psychological entity, an act of altruistic love. Since we can love more than we know, those whose view of reality is, through no fault of their own, erroneous can still love. The absolutely essential cognitive base of community, as a result, is not religion, and not metaphysics, but sincerity in regard to one's convictions. The content of the convictions about which one is sincere will be, to some extent, beside the point. If he is sincere, an atheist, an agnostic, a contractarian, even, might be able to identify with his fellows in altruistic love, and thereby appropriate the entire community of being, even while professing not to do so. But his sincerity, as we shall see, must meet certain carefully defined conditions. And those conditions will put him on the road, if not to religious belief, then to some equivalent of a creationist metaphysics. For sincerity necessarily implies a belief in, and the reality of, some transcendent entity that establishes a community prior to all human choices and convictions.

The dictionary meaning of *sincere* is, of course, "honest, truthful, being the same in actuality as in outward appearance." The term is derived from a Latin phrase, "*sine cere*," "without wax." The phrase originally referred to Roman coins which were truly worth what they appeared to be worth, coins in which the metal had not been adulterated with wax. A sincere person, then, is one in whom interior and exterior coincide. He is someone who really is what he appears to be, who really does believe what he professes to believe. Sincerity in a person, however, implies a paradoxical and delicate balance between two mental states that seem to contradict each other. A sincere person holds fast to his convictions, no matter what the price. But at the same time, he is willing to give them up at a moment's notice. How can such attitudes be combined? How does his strong adherence to his beliefs fit with what looks like a tentative, provisional grasp of them?

The answer is not that he hedges his bets by holding back from a whole-hearted commitment. Such a person would not be sincere, but a hypocrite. A sincere person commits his mind entirely to his convictions, and holds to them no matter what the price. He is, in fact, willing to die for them. If his convictions became inconvenient, say, or carried a social

penalty, he would still hold to them. If he were threatened
with death for his beliefs, he would still hold to them. If he
were offered high rewards for giving them up, he would still
hold them tight. One who gives up his convictions because of
inconvenience, ostracism, or even death is not sincere. Nor is
he who holds them for ulterior motives – social status, money,
power. He who holds certain convictions only as long as the
price is right is not sincere but a hypocrite. A willingness
to put a price on his convictions – any price – would show
that he held them for some self-serving motive. But to a
sincere person, his convictions are beyond all price. Like
all the best things in life, they are priceless. He holds to
them because they are true, not because they are convenient,
popular, rewarding, or even protective of his life. He who is
without wax adheres to the truth, for the sake of the truth.
Truth is his supreme value, a higher value than life itself.

But the sincere person's willingness to give up his most
treasured beliefs at a moment's notice – under certain conditions – is an equally important part of his sincerity. One
who clings to his opinions no matter what evidence he finds
to the contrary is not sincere, but a fanatic. One who would
suffer ostracism, even death, for ideas and principles that are
patently false is not sincere. The sincere person, holding his
convictions because they are true – and for no other reason
– willingly gives them up as soon as he sees them to be false.
But a fanatic does not. In other words, the apparent paradox
of solid commitment along with an equally firm detachment
is resolved by the sincere person's motive for holding his convictions: their truth. Given that, he will pay any price, even
death. But absent that, he will pay no price at all. What
is not true has no hold on him whatsoever. Just as he will
not give up his convictions, not for any price, neither will he
assume them for any price. Truth is his only criterion.

All sincere people, then – no matter what it is that they
are sincere about – take truth as the standard by which they
measure their own minds and govern their lives. All have, as
the motivation for their commitment to their convictions, a
love for truth as some sort of supreme value, dearer even than
life itself. In fact, for sincere people, life without truth has no
value. But such an attitude toward truth – and there can be
no sincerity without it – carries certain implications. The first
is that truth must be some sort of concrete reality, not a mere
abstraction, not a mere construct of our minds, not relative
to or dependent on our choices and judgments. Truth is a real
entity, not a fiction. For it would be folly, indeed, to give one's

life – or to pay any price at all, even the least inconvenience – for a mere abstraction. What the mind constructs, the mind can annihilate. And so, if truth as an abstraction became inconvenient, painful, or fatal, the intelligent, rational person would simply change the construct. Rational persons do not allow mere abstractions to make any demands on them at all, let alone the final demand. The logic of sincerity, then, requires that truth be a concrete reality.

But then, truth as a concrete reality which can command our assent, and make demands on us, including the final demand, must have some other features, too. It must be real in some transcendent way – beyond all human minds, beyond our control and manipulation. We must submit to it. And so, it is superior to us in its degree of reality. It is a higher kind of being. And as such a higher being, truth is a criterion not just for our minds but for our actions as well. For in seeking truth, in deciding our convictions and verifying them, we make choices about our behavior. Truth must be able to impose some sort of sanction on us. Truth – with a capital T – must be in some sense independent of us and yet something that we need to be in union with, for our own fully flourishing existence. Such an entity – real, concrete, transcendent, having dominion over us – has at least these essential characteristics of the God of all believers and of the Creator of our communal metaphysics. Thus all sincere persons are implicitly traveling on the road to belief. They may not reason to a One as the source of the many, to Being as omnipresent cause of being. They may not go so far as to admit to a personal God, the Lord of History. But at least they view Truth as some sort of a real entity that is higher than their minds and sovereign over their lives. Otherwise, they would be ideologues, fanatics, hypocrites, or all of these.

There is a basis for community, then, apart from Biblical faith and apart from an explicit creationist metaphysics, on the part of all people who hold sincerely to any convictions whatsoever. Submission to truth requires the existence of truth as the transcendent unifier of all its adherents. Truth serves as the unifying factor, prior to communal love, by which sincere persons can identify with each other, making each other each other's other self. The commitment to Truth, to a transcendent reality which commands our loyalties, thus presupposes a community similar to the community of being. All sincere persons are united to truth as their common goal and exemplar, and thus are united with each other. They form a community of inquiry which, while unified, totally respects the individuality and diversity of all its members. Many are one in the tentative commitment, the committed tentativeness, by which each submits his mind to various convictions, only because they are true. Each devotes himself to his convictions with a readiness to give them up if they should prove false. But all other inquiries, all other convictions, have the potential to prove them false. Hence, each inquirer respects completely the individuality and the integrity of every other inquirer in his unique, sincere search for truth. And yet all adhere tenaciously to Truth as their goal and criterion. And so, inquirers are both one and many, a community in which many are turned into one without ceasing to be many. Tenuous in their inquiry, they are many, each with his individual integrity as a searcher. All respect that integrity in the others. But tenacious in their convictions, they are one in their common submission to Truth as a single, transcendent reality. All respect that commitment in the others, thus identifying with them in altruistic love.

What, then, is the tie that binds in the community of sincere truthseekers? It is, prior to any conscious search for community, the Truth which all seek, even from each other. It is, in appropriating that community, the altruistic love by which an inquirer would identify another inquirer as his other self, wish for him the full flourishing of his sincere inquiry as it is suited to his individuality, and wish that fullness to him for his sake rather than for the lover's own. Such a lover would thereby make his friend's sincerity his own, so that the two would be bound together by the possession of a single good in common, the single transcendent Truth which grounds their diverse inquiries. The lover would possess as his own the Truth to which he and his friend were jointly committed, as well as his friend's sincere inquiry. And since that Truth is one and the same for all sincere inquirers, he would immediately come into community with all other sincere inquirers, of all times and all places. For the community of inquiry, the community unified by Truth as its "*fons et origo*," is a whole, as is the community of being. And that community is either appropriated in its entirety, or it is not appropriated at all.

Sincerity, then, implies tolerance, in the strongest possible sense of that term. Tolerance is but the particular form taken by altruistic love when one sincere person affirms and supports the search for truth wherever he finds it – in others loved for their sakes, and in himself as well. As in the case of any altruistic love, his support for the inquiry of other sin-

cere persons coincides with self-love. It is not in opposition
to his love for his own sincere search, nor in some kind of
compromising balance with it. A sincere search for truth –
a search which combines an absolute and wholehearted commitment to what one's best effort shows to be true, with an
instant willingness to withdraw that commitment once evidence leads the other way – is but an added way of being
the unified individuals that we are. In tolerating each other's
inquiries, we appropriate the community of Truth that exists
among us prior to our love for each other. All sincere inquirers, then, can realize community. They need not be religious
believers. They need not hold a creationist metaphysics, at
least not explicitly. They might be atheistic humanists. But
they must be devoted to truth.[28]

Sincerity, then, in whatever anyone holds as true, is an
absolute requirement for his being an altruistic lover, and
thus for being a communal person. Without such sincerity,
there is no commitment to Truth, and thus no prior unity
which would allow him to identify another inquirer as his
other self. But anyone who takes truth as a criterion for
his thought and his life, thus implicitly submitting himself
to transcendent Truth, is thereby a member of a community
that transcends time and space. That community is, first of
all, a community of all of those who share his convictions –
past, present, and future. But his existential communion extends beyond them to include all sincere inquirers into truth,
as well as the Truth to which all are united. All he need do
in order to realize that community within himself is to love
any one inquirer altruistically. For to love one is to love all.
And to fail to love one is to fail to love all.

We can see the difference between such a community and
a mere contractual association in an example – say, the group
of scholars who specialize in the history of the Industrial Revolution.[29]   A sincere inquirer into that complex historical
event seeks to know the truth about it. He does not invent,
distort, or conceal data in order to advance his career or increase his income. He tries to find out the exact truth and to

---

[28] Tinder provides a fine analysis of tolerance, as an instance of the love that builds
community among sincere inquirers, in Chapter V of *Community, Reflections on a
Tragic Ideal.* See "In Defense of Pure Tolerance," pp. 78-100.

[29] This view of scholarship as a communal, because loving, inquiry into truth was
powerfully suggested by John Nef's "Is the Intellectual Life an End in Itself?" in *The
Review of Politics, XXIV,* 1962, pp. 3-18. Nef concludes with a negative answer to
his question: "It is not the intellectual life, it is love that is an end in itself" (p. 18).

communicate it lovingly to his fellows, whatever such communication might cost him, financially, or otherwise. In thus taking Truth as his criterion, and in loving his fellow inquirers, he becomes one ontologically with all other historians of the Industrial Revolution, of all times and places. He realizes, appropriates, a community that includes all his fellows – those he associates with, those he reads, those for whom he writes, those whom he never comes to know.

And yet, the ontological union of these scholars, appropriated as it is by everyone who partakes of it in altruistic love, is no threat to the individuality of any of its members. Each is free, and is lovingly encouraged, to seek the truth according to his unique talents and interests. The members of this community prize each other's talents and opportunities, and share their results, in a total generosity. Each identifies the others' flourishing as his own, and thus comes into communion with it. Such scholars do not compete for prestige, for grants and other research opportunities, for income and promotions. Instead, they cooperate in seeking these benefits for each other. As they associate with each other in love, the paradoxical logic of their altruism follows its inevitable course. They find their fulfillment in self-sacrifice. They are glad to see resources allotted in the ways that best promote their common inquiry. They are, in fact, ready and willing to give up their scholarly lives for each other, if circumstances should make that step the best way to promote the communal inquiry into the Truth, of which the truth about the Industrial Revolution is but a part.

A mere contractual association of Industrial Revolution historians, on the other hand, would have quite different relationships, even if they followed the very same procedures in their work, in their allocation of resources, in their sharing of their results, and so on. The crucial element, as always, is their motives for their association with each other. If their motives are utilitarian or hedonistic (or both), as contractual motives always are, their motivations will also be egocentric. Such scholars will enjoy none of the unity found in a community of scholars who identify with each other in altruistic love. The scholars of a contractual association may, to varying degrees, prize each other's individual differences, support each other's work, share their results – but each for the sake of his own use and pleasure. As each one is centered on his own private good, the many possess no single good in common. They enjoy only the appearance of unity with each other, not the existential reality of community. The tie that binds is not formed among them.

In a crisis, the logic of these contrasting motives will tell. When scholarly associations are merely contractual, some of these scholars, when pressured to choose between their own advancement and the communal inquiry into truth, will begin to invent or falsify data. They will be competitive rather than cooperative in seeking grants, teaching positions and assignments, publishing opportunities, promotions, and so on. They will see the research of others as a threat to their own, and will then look for ways to inhibit the work of others so that they themselves may prosper. The truth of the Industrial Revolution is not a primary value for them, nor do they prize the talents of their fellow researchers. When cooperation is to their private advantage, they will cooperate. When it is not, they will not. Their spirit was epitomized by one scholar, emerging from a session at a convention who said, "Wasn't that neat the way So-and-so shot him down? And he hadn't even read his paper!"

As these contractually related scholars continue to associate with each other, the logic of their egocentric motives will follow its inevitable course. Having no basis on which to sacrifice themselves for each other, they do not do so. They are not happy to see resources go to anyone other than themselves. Any thought of giving up their scholarly lives for each other is out of the question. When they do give up some benefit for themselves – a grant, a teaching opportunity, time off for research – they do so because they see some greater advantage to themselves in so doing. They do not support each other's commitment to Truth as a transcendent reality, for there is no such commitment to support. The results, as with any egocentric motivation, go beyond their ontological isolation from each other and from researchers of the past and future. For the logic of their motives is the implicitly murderous logic of any egocentric association. Should some crisis lead them to withdraw support from their fellows in order to enhance their own self-primacy, their association, which will have been only an apparent unity from the start, will disintegrate. Their competition will become cutthroat. They will destroy each other's scholarly lives.

In the final analysis, then, our fundamental motives have their effects on our actions. Why we do what we do eventually determines what we do as well. Scholars of any speciality who live by contractarian principles are mere associates. No matter how genteel and polite they may be in their outward behavior, they are inwardly competitive and hostile to each other. Lacking any truly unifying bond, they remain detached individuals. Side-by-side when that posture is beneficial for themselves, they are face-to-face in open conflict when it is not. They lack a common relationship to a transcendent reality that could unite them. Their very association with each other threatens their individuality, and their individuality constantly threatens their association. Their ties to each other are not existential, but only external. To the extent that they do love each other, they reduce each other to abstractions. Their love is selective and conditional, and they treat each other as objects, as mere means, as things rather than persons. Their ontological isolation, then, is complete.

People who are to be linked precisely as they are, as individuals, as concrete wholes who are diverse from each other in their existence, can form a community only if they are related to some one reality that transcends them all. The God of the Bible is one such reality, as is the Creator of an existential metaphysics. Truth can be a similar unifying reality, as those who submit to it in sincere inquiry then have a communality which they can appropriate in altruistic love. Those who inquire into the truth of some particular part of the world, such as the Industrial Revolution, have a basis for community in their commitment to Truth. But the realization of community depends totally on the motives with which they associate with each other. Thus a commitment to Truth can serve, as well as love of the Biblical God, or of the metaphysical Creator, as a tie that binds, a tie which altruistic love can then reduplicate.

Given these conclusions, we can suggest several possible bases for genuine community. But all such bases must meet one criterion: any basis for genuine community must consist in some prior link of its potential members to a common transcendent reality. That link constitutes a real communality which its members can then appropriate in altruistic love. But then, the realization of community will depend entirely on the motives of its participants. Those who love altruistically will be in community with those whom they love and, implicitly, at least, with all others who share the common bond to the transcendent reality in question. To affirm any one person's existence as it flows from the Creator is to affirm the existence of all, and thus to come into community with all. Likewise, to affirm anyone's sincere inquiry into truth is to implicitly affirm everyone else's as well, and thus to come into community with all sincere inquirers.

We can think of many other possible bases for community. All who sincerely seek justice, for example, or live for love, all those who make community itself their life goal – such people partake, in their sincerity, in a common relationship to a single transcendent reality, and that participation constitutes a communality that they can appropriate in altruistic love. In fact, what such people seek, if they are sincere, is the truth about justice, about love and community. What they seek is the reality of that truth, its actual existence in the world. And so, a sincere commitment to truth is the fundamental basis on which many other goals can lead to genuine community. Atheisms of several varieties, including secular humanism, might ground genuine community in the minds and hearts of those who sincerely deny any God or afterlife. But atheists, of course, must meet the test of sincerity. And in their sincerity, they will implicitly affirm what they explicitly deny. For any loyalty to truth implies the existence of Truth, Truth as a transcendent reality which can demand our lives. Such a reality has the essential features of a Creator, of the Biblical God. Thus secularism, and atheism, when they are sincere, implicitly transcend themselves and are on the way to becoming, if not religious belief, at least a metaphysical theism.

Part of sincerity, then, is being open to the unsuspected implications of what we explicitly believe. Being open to implications implies, in its turn, being willing to convert our motives. An openness to Truth and a willingness to be converted to altruism are thus part of sincerity wherever it is found, the sincerity that is the essential ground for any community whatsoever. Sincerity, then, is a criterion by which we distinguish genuine communities from contracts, from mere associations. We honor many groupings of people with the title *community.* Are we right to do so? What about the business community? The gay community? The black community? The academic community? These, and all others as well, are authentic communities for those of their members who are sincerely devoted to Truth and altruistically motivated in their actions toward their fellows. The business community, for example, might really exist, at least for some businessmen. There is no reason why the making and buying and selling of goods cannot be done lovingly, as part of a sincere inquiry into the truth of things and an altruistic love of one's fellows. One need not be driven by the profit motive in order to make a profit. Those who associate in business need not be mere business associates.

But there are some limits to sincerity. There is a minimal content to the convictions that any person can be sincerely committed to. That content will be spelled out more completely in a later chapter. But an example can make the present point. Take a radically individualistic view of human persons, in which we are conceived as atomic, detached units – the view of social contract theory. Such a view leaves no basis for the identification in love that produces the tie that binds us into genuine community. Such individualism is epitomized in the slogan that is often urged to justify abortion on demand: "A woman has the right to do what she wants with her own body." Apart from all questions as to whose body a fetus is, what are the implications of this slogan? Clearly, it says that what a woman wants to do is what she has a right to do. She need not consult anyone else, not even the father of her fetus. She decides, as a wholly private individual, with no attachments to anyone else. But if we explore the logic of her slogan, we see contradictions within it that make it an impossible premise for anyone who sincerely inquires into truth.

First of all, we can say what we say to our children when they take each other's toys: "You wouldn't like it if somebody did that to you. So don't you do it, either." The slogan cannot be universalized as a moral principle. For if a woman has a right to do what she wants with her own body, then so does a rapist, a murderer, a thief, even someone who feels like poking his finger into someone else's eye. But further, even if we consider only a woman as a single individual, she cannot operate out of such a principle. A woman has no right to use her body to drive someone else's car away, to stick a knife in the ribs of a passer-by, to forge a check, or to poke her finger in someone else's eye. There are many restrictions on what a woman can do with her own body, restrictions that the most individualistic among us accept. The slogan is simply absurd as a principle of human behavior.

Given some minimal content to which any sincere mind must be committed, and other content which lies beyond the pale of sincere inquiry, there are many complexities and ambiguities in the ways in which human beings seek the truth and associate with each other. Thus, community can and does happen in many different ways. To return to our sincere historian of the Industrial Revolution, he does not selectively seek the truth in love, in his scholarly work but not in the rest of his life. He does so in all of his daily life, as do the masses of people who are not scholars in any field. In fact, anyone's honest curiosity about anything – the weather, baseball scores, the number of shirts in his third drawer – is a search for objective truth. We don't want arbitrary, comfortable opinions on these matters. We want to know what the weather is, what the baseball scores are, how many shirts really are in the third drawer. In this simple desire for the daily truth about the way things are, we are implicitly using as a criterion for our convictions the Truth that transcends all of our minds. In much of daily life, we all live by that one Truth.

This daily sincerity may seem unimportant, but it is the stuff of our daily fulfillment, of our continuous ontological healing. Our adherence to Truth is what makes any conversation – any communication – possible. We can ask each other questions, about anything, with some real possibility of trusting each other's answers, only because we can measure those answers by a single, real criterion that transcends any human manipulation. It is in submission to that Truth that we live, and move, and have our being. It is not just scholars in a given field, then, who are unified in their common loyalty to a single standard of truth. All of us humans, in every moment of our seeking to know "how it is with being," accept the conditions necessary for making that search. Without a profound common loyalty to truth, we would have no sincerity. And then the simplest moment of curiosity, the plainest effort to communicate, would not be possible.

A group of hypocrites may exchange words, then, but they cannot communicate with each other. They can only emit streams of sound which each one aims at his own self-primacy, as he seeks approval, prestige, power, and safety for himself through the manipulation of the other members of the group that he belongs to. The same is true of an association of fanatics. They cannot converse about anything. They also cling to their opinions with a motivation that is egocentric. But people who are sincere can converse. And when they do, no matter how ordinary their subject-matter, they appropriate the community of being in altruistic love. For such love is the immediate corollary to sincerity. A sincere person presumes his fellows to be sincere until he has evidence to the contrary. In so doing, he loves them. And in his love, community comes to be.

Communication depends on this basic trust. When we presume that someone is a sincere person, and not a hypocrite or a fanatic, we pay him an enormous compliment. That compliment is our altruistic love, a love by which we affirm and rejoice in his submission to Truth. In this simple, daily trust, we identify with our fellowmen in their inquiry, wishing its continuation for their sakes. We do not just look on them as possible sources of useful or pleasant information for ourselves. If we were to do so, we would lapse into an egocentric association that would immediately make community impossible. If such egocentric motives were the prevailing ones in our daily life, trust would disintegrate to the point that even our polite contractual associations with each other would collapse. We face life-or-death choices, then, in our casual comments about the weather, in our purchasing of our newspapers, in all the daily acts by which we show a basic trust in each other. In those seemingly trivial and mundane actions, we are moved by motives that ultimately imply either self-sacrifice or murder.

What we trust is, precisely, each other's sincere submission to Truth, a submission that makes us one while leaving us many. In trusting that submission, and supporting it in each other, for each other's sakes, we form community. For in that ordinary daily altruism, all the implications of love unfold. We appropriate the entire community of being, even as we implicitly offer our lives to each other and for each other. We appropriate the natural communality that is ours as members of the community of inquiry. This pre-reflective sincerity saves us from hypocrisy and fanaticism. By the paradoxical nature of sincerity, which combines a willingness to die for our convictions with an instant readiness to give them up, religious believers and atheists have a common ground, and thus the possibility of community with each other.

By the same token, even communal thinkers and contractarians might find a common ground, provided only that both are sincere. For a sincere denial of community, premised as it must be on an affirmation of Truth, is an implicit affirmation of the community that is denied. If someone is sincerely convinced that contractual relations are the only possible ones, he is willing to die for that conviction, and to pay lesser prices as well, simply because it is true. But at the very moment when he makes Truth his supreme value, dearer even than life itself, he takes his first step away from his contractarian convictions. He finds common ground for conversation with his fellows. He has a rational basis for altruistic cooperation with them. But most importantly, he is already ontologically healed. He appropriates the community that is already a fact. Love is folded into his sincere denial of it.

In our common adherence to truth, then, we find the
roots of love. For every sincere person supports the sincerity
of his fellows, for their sakes. Their inquiries could lead him
to the truth that he seeks. Thus is community engendered
in each and every encounter between people who are sincere.
The logic of sincerity leads inevitably to community, even as
the logic of hypocrisy and fanaticism lead away from it.

Richard Leakey's recent research into human origins has
unearthed some plausible evidence that this basic daily trust
was the earliest human trait to evolve – even before language,
religion, or the use of fire to cook food.[30]   From his calculations of the population of the earliest humans, and of their
food supply, Leakey has concluded that the first men simply
would not have survived unless they had done something that
no animals of other species have been known to do. They regularly shared their food with each other, adults voluntarily
feeding other adults. Other animals hunt for food in pairs or
in packs, but when they find it, each adult feeds itself and,
perhaps, its young. But the earliest men, in a simple gesture
scarcely one step above an animal instinct, regularly fed each
other. It is easy to see in that simple gesture all the elements
of trust, of identification, and of the altruistic love that constitute community. Food-sharing was their appropriation of
the community of being.

In order to see these communal implications, we need
only imagine ourselves in the place of these first humans.
Their day-in, day-out occupation was to find enough food
for their survival. When one of them found some food, he
did not know whether he or his fellows would ever find any
more. He could have, then, hoarded it to himself. He could
have taken away the food found by his weaker fellows, even
killed them. He could have at least eaten to his fill and then
moved on, showing no concern for anyone else. And yet, he
did none of these things. In a remarkable, unspoken altruism,
he turned at once to share his find with his fellows.

That sharing, prior even to language, was but a slight
step above animal instinct. Certainly it could not have been
a contractual contrivance by minds which had not yet learned
to symbolize their thoughts in words or pictures. Nor was it
explicit religious belief. But it was the evolution of a distinc-

---

[30] See Richard E. Leakey and Roger Lewin, *Origins: What New Discoveries Reveal
About the Emergence of Our Species and Its Possible Future* (New York, E. P. Dutton,
1977), pp. 10-11, 116-117 and 148-150.

tively human behavior. And that small step was a crucial one. For it is one man's trusting identification with another that is at the heart of any community. Each primitive man who shared his food was seeing his fellow as his other self, wishing for him what he would wish for himself, and wishing it to him for his sake. Each saw his neighbor as a person rather than a thing, and loved him with an unconditional love, as an absolute rather than a relative value. Each primitive food-sharer thus came into communion with his beloved other self. In that simple, unspoken communion, we can see his appropriation of the entire community of being, with all its implications for the healing of his ontological loneliness. *Homo sapiens* was willing to give up his life for his friend, and actually did so, as surely as if he had stepped into the path of a charging wild beast. In the simple gesture of sharing food, the world's first secular humanists transformed the animal instinct for self-preservation into the reality of community.

CHAPTER VI
COMMUNITY AND ACTION

If Leakey's interpretation of his evidence is correct, the earliest men displayed several important features of genuine community. In sharing their food they exercised what is essential for community to be real – the inward attitude that constitutes altruistic love. For community is fundamentally an interior reality, and even when it is nothing more than that, community can be completely real. Outward actions, speech, even, are not absolutely necessary for the enactment of community. Thus an invalid, a paralytic who cannot even speak or nod or blink his eyes, can come into as full an appropriation of the community of being as does anyone else. All he needs to do is to love someone altruistically. In such hidden, interior love he makes community real and finds his full ontological healing.

But outward actions, the speaking of love and acting it out in the practical realm, can also be important. Leakey's primitives illustrate perfectly how intention and praxis are connected. Those who found food could hardly have a sincere interior love for their fellows without actually giving them what they needed to eat in order to survive. On the face of it, then, community has some obvious implications for praxis, for action in the world of time and space. But the complex of relations between community and action are not all immediately clear. We need first to understand the particular kind of outward actions that can be communal. We need also to consider the relations between inward intentions and outward actions. In exploring these topics, we will see that community is a moral matter, that community even becomes our norm for deciding between right and wrong, good and evil, in human behavior.

Thus, community comes to be a tie that binds us in a second way, a duty, obligation, and norm. The tie that binds us ontologically binds us morally as well. It obliges us to love. Community, with its intrinsic logic and ontology, bears an intrinsic relation to ethics as well. The discernment of good and evil in moral life will lead us to an examination of communal failures, i.e. to see what becomes of communal intentions, and of the reality of community itself, when our best efforts at praxis fall short. The question of evil – of evil members in a community, of whole communities of evil-doers – is also important. At the end of all these considerations,

we will conclude that community is exactly identical with
the moral good, so that morally right actions are those that
build community. A corollary will be that an evil community,
a community of evil-doers, is metaphysically impossible, as
is even one evil person's membership in community. For the
appropriation of the community of being in altruistic love is
identical with right moral action and decision.[31]   To do a
moral wrong is *ipso facto* to isolate oneself from community.

Altruistic love is a distinctively human activity. Though
other animals seem to sacrifice themselves for each other,
they act instinctively, impulsively – not by the conscious, self-
reflective free choice that is characteristic of humans. Even
Leakey's primitives were advanced beyond the other animals
in this important respect. They acted with a self-awareness
that not only told them what they were doing, but also that
they did not have to do it. They could have done otherwise.
We humans do, of course, act instinctively and impulsively
at times, as do the other animals. And some of our activities
are not conscious at all – the many biochemical processes
that our bodies perform in the course of a day, for example,
and our response to gravity and other physical forces as we
go about our daily business.

But altruistic love, and thus all outward actions that generate community, belong to a class of activities known as deliberate acts, or free choices. In order to see the connections
between interior communal acts and the outward enacting of
them, we need to take a closer look at the process of deliberation. Sometimes deliberation is so quick and easy that we
do not notice it. At other times, it is difficult, complex, time-
consuming – maybe even an occasion for seeking counsel. In
any case, the basic structure is the same in all deliberate acts.
Thanks to that structure, all communal acts, which are by
definition deliberate, have some common features.

The first common feature, indicated in the derivation of
the term *deliberate* from the Latin *liber*, meaning "free," is
freedom. Deliberate acts are those that we need not do. They
are under our control, and so we do not perform them unless
we choose to do so. Accordingly, they are actions for which
we are responsible, or answerable, for which we deserve to be
rewarded or punished. When someone asks, "Why did this

---

[31] This analysis of deliberate action and the moral responsibility that results from
it is derived from Aquinas' treatise on moral acts in *S. Th.* I-II. He identifies the moral
good with the human existential good at I-II, 18, "Whether Every Human Action is
Good, or Are There Evil Actions?"

happen?" if it happened by my deliberate activity, then I
must answer for it. I must claim the action as my own, or
own up to it. It belongs to me because I am its only cause.
If I cook a meal for my family, for example, the cooking was
entirely in my power. It did not have to happen. I could
have chosen not to do it. But since I did make it happen,
I am responsible, or answerable, for it. If I did it lovingly,
one of its results is community – my own appropriation of
the community of being. Since the one who is responsible for
an action is also responsible for its results, I am responsible
for that community, too. I can own up to it because I own
it. Whatever credit is due, whatever praise or other reward,
whatever gratitude – all are due to me, as consequences of
my free choice.

Besides being free and responsible, deliberate actions are
also intentional. Before we enact them, we intend them. We
literally "stretch out" toward them with our minds and wills.
Often enough, we intend certain actions as means to an end.
They are "on the mean," midway between ourselves and the
end that is the goal or purpose of those actions. I might cook
a meal as a means to my children's growth. In that case, I
meant to do it. Some ends are intermediate. That is, they
are means, in their turn, to some further goal or purpose. I
may cook so that my son might grow so that he might win a
wrestling meet so that he will gain a college scholarship, and
so on, through a whole series of intermediate ends.

The series of means intended for ends which are intended
as means to further ends cannot, however, be endless. There
must be, at least implicitly, some goal or purpose that is an
ultimate end, not a means to some further goal or purpose.
For my intention of an end is the reason for my deliberately
choosing a means to it. Without a desire for my family to
eat, I will not be moved to cook for them. If I didn't want
my son to grow, I wouldn't wish him to eat. If I didn't want
him to wrestle, I wouldn't be concerned for his growing – and
so on. The difference between a means and an end is that
an end is sought for its own sake, while a means is sought
for the sake of the end to which it leads. Intermediate ends
are sought for the sake of further ends. Thus, if all ends
were intermediate, and none of them ultimate, I would have
no reason to seek any of the ends or means in my series.
I would, then, do nothing, because there would be nothing
I would really intend to do. At the root of all intentional,
deliberate actions is some ultimate end that is willed for its
own sake, purely as an end in itself and not as a means to

anything further. I may not consciously advert to it every time I act, but it must be implicitly present. Otherwise I am acting unintentionally. What I do then happens accidentally, not by my intention. And accidental actions do not build community. The identification of another as my other self, the very heart of the love that generates community, has, as its deliberately intended ultimate end, the well-being of my beloved.

These distinctively human actions, the ones that are deliberate and intentional, and thus aimed at some ultimate end, make up the category of moral activity. They are actions that have moral significance, that can be right or wrong, good or evil. The history of language reveals this connection. Our term *moral* is derived from the Latin *mores*, which mean "customs." But customs are distinctive to human beings. They are, unlike the instinctive behavior of animals, freely chosen patterns of behavior that become typical of a culture because elders choose, freely, to pass them on to the young. But the derivation of *mores* is even more revealing. It comes from the Greek, *maiesthai*, meaning "to try." Deliberate acts are not those that we do unintentionally, without trying. They are those in which we strive for some outcome as the goal, purpose, or end of our activity. When we try to do something, we intend some end and take deliberate steps to achieve it. But what we achieve without trying brings us no credit, no thanks or praise, no responsibility. Responsibility, credit, praiseworthiness, gratitude – these are all moral entities, the results of deliberate actions. And so is community. Altruistic love is no accident.

Since everything we do deliberately has an ultimate end, we can divide all of our moral acts into two basic kinds. For the ultimate end of every action is either our own individualistic welfare or that of another, our private self or a beloved other self. The ultimate end of an action is what we have referred to in previous chapters as motivation. A motive, as the term itself indicates, is what moves us to act when we need not do so, and to act in one way rather than any of the other ways in which we might have acted. To return to our example, when I cook for my son, his college scholarship is not my ultimate end. Ultimately I want him to have that scholarship for one of two reasons: his welfare as a person, or some benefit to myself, such as my own prestige, my own sense of success or control, perhaps, or his ability to care for me in my old age. My motive, in other words, is either altruistic or egocentric. My cooking, then, either builds com-

munity or destroys it, depending on the ultimate end I have
in mind when I decide to do it. That ultimate end, my motive, is "what I'm really after," "what I really want to get out
of this." It is where my will is finally centered or focused.

All deliberate acts, then, are either communal or anti-
communal, depending on whether they are altruistically or
egocentrically motivated, whether their ultimate end is the
isolated good of the self or the good of the beloved, the other
self. Moral acts thus divide into two kinds: morally right or
good, and morally wrong or evil. The first – altruistic – are
those that we ought to do. They fit with the kind of beings
that we are. The others – egocentric – do not sort well with
our nature. They are actions that we ought not do. It isn't
fitting or suitable for one with a communal nature to act con-
trariwise. Community, then, which is the deliberate appropriation of our communal being, is the standard by which we
measure the moral goodness of our deliberate actions. Community is the norm of morality. What fosters community is
morally right and good. What fosters egocentric solitude is
wrong, morally evil. The act of cooking a meal can be either,
depending on the ultimate end for which I do it. Egocentric
cooking is morally evil because it destroys community. But
altruistic cooking is a way to build community, and is thereby
morally right and good.

The moral good, then, is one kind of ontological good,
the distinctively human. It brings our existential fulfillment,
heals our ontological loneliness. The moral good is the ontological good that is proper to human beings, a free and
conscious appropriation of the community of being by one
who freely and consciously recognizes his natural place in
that community. Our moral goodness, the virtue which Aristotle saw as the basis of genuine friendships, is nothing more
than our fully flourishing existence as the kind of beings that
we are – ontologically lonely and yet capable of transcending
ourselves by deliberately appropriating the entire community
of being. In a way, our human goodness, moral goodness, is
like the goodness of any other kind of being in the world. An
apple tree is a good apple tree when it reaches its existential fullness. A good apple tree achieves its correct shape,
size, and function – the production of apples. A bad tree
is a defective tree, one that lacks some of its distinctive existential fullness. It may be stunted or sterile, thus falling
short of what it might be. Similarly, a good person is one
who reaches his existential fullness, who comes to be all that
he can be. He is one who, in deliberate acts which have as

their ultimate end the welfare of a beloved other, appropriates the entire community of being. An evil man is one who fails in that appropriation. He exists less fully than he might because his deliberate actions have as their ultimate end his individualistic self. Such a person is stunted in his very existence, much as a tree that fails to reach its full height. Moral goodness, then, coincides with the healing of the ontological loneliness of human beings. It is nothing else but community. Moral evil, on the other hand, coincides with the deliberate reinforcement of one's ontological loneliness. It is nothing else but the failure to appropriate community.

Our deepest moral choices, then, have to do not so much with what we do as with why we do what we do. They have to do with ends rather than means, with motives rather than actions. For we choose certain actions only because we have already intended certain ends. And those ends determine our moral identities, the kind of persons that we are. There comes a moment in the life of every moral adult when, for the first time, he explicitly thinks about some overall goal or purpose for his life. Once he begins to intend that goal as an ultimate end, he makes many other decisions about how to act, taking that ultimate goal as his norm. For example, he might decide upon competitive money-making as the ultimate purpose of his life. Money would then be his supreme good, and everything else would be evaluated in terms of that. Money would be the norm or standard by which he would decide what he ought to do. He would then decide whether or not to marry, and even whom to marry, on the basis of which course of action would take him toward his money-making goals. His wife would then be a means to his economic end. Every time he had to make a decision – about where to live and work, whether and when to have children, whether and with whom to form friendships – his decisions would be based on the means that would best further his money-making goals. As long as money-making remained his ultimate end, he would subordinate everything else to it. He would give up his health and his social life, his friends and family in order to pursue his profits, if these sacrifices became necessary.

When we select our ultimate ends, then, we do much more than set ourselves on the course of one particular action. We determine the degree of our own ontological fulfillment. We decide how real we are going to be, how far our existence is going to extend. These fundamental choices are always either communal or anti-communal, for our ultimate ends are always either the good of those we identify as our

other selves or the good of our solitary selves. All of our
deliberate actions are either means or intermediate ends ordered to one of these two ultimate ends. And they are to be
judged good or evil in terms of the goodness and evil of those
ultimate ends. If our ultimate end is communal, our motive
altruistic, then all deliberate actions which are means to that
end are morally right and good. Conversely, if our ultimate
end is anti-communal, our motive egocentric, then all deliberate actions which are means to that end are morally wrong
and evil.

Community is thus the norm for many decisions – indeed, for all decisions. Vocational choices, decisions about
marrying or not, and with whom, choices about what kind
of education to pursue, and where and when to pursue it –
all of these are moral decisions. All of them, and all other
deliberate choices, involve actions which will either build or
destroy community, depending on the ultimate end toward
which we direct them. Community is, indeed, the norm for
all of human life. It is the guide to right decisions about work
and play, about family life and education, about political and
military activity. Community is the norm for decisions about
medical care and business, about war and peace. For whenever a human person acts deliberately, intentionally, seeking
some goal or purpose, he makes a basic option. He orients
himself toward one of two ultimate ends. Thus, whenever
anyone makes a decision about anything, he is either appropriating or refusing the community of being. The communal
alternative is always morally right and good, and the anti-
communal one evil and wrong. Community is the ultimate
norm or standard of morality.

We can now draw several conclusions about the relations
between community and action. The first has to do with
the connections between community as an interior state, or
the intention of another's good as the ultimate end, and the
outward, practical enactment of that intention in the world
of time, space, and material entities. It may seem that ultimate ends are all that matter, that once I intend community
as an ultimate end, I automatically achieve it. For community is an interior entity. But such is not the case. To return to our primitive food-sharers, was their mere intention
to protect each other's physical life from starvation enough
to constitute them a community? After all, community becomes real in the first moment of altruistic love. To love any
one person is, implicitly, to appropriate the entire community of being. Did the actual sharing of food add anything

essential to the community that they already enjoyed in their
intention? What if they tried to find food for each other and
failed, due to circumstances beyond their control? What if
one of them tried instead to find a private hoard and make
a stockpile for himself, only to end up sharing the food unintentionally when the others found his stockpile and ate it?
Does unintended practical success build community? Does
unintended practical failure destroy community? Does exterior success add anything important to the interior reality
that community essentially consists in? How is action related
to the psychological entity constituted by love?[32]

The answers to these questions can be surmised from a
simple premise, one that is derived from the nature of sincerity. In brief, sincere altruistic intentions lead to sincere
best efforts in the practical realm; but when best efforts fail,
community is still achieved in its full reality. Good intentions
are necessary but not adequate, except when good intentions
are all that is practically possible, in which case they are adequate. Since communal actions are moral actions, they are
essentially acts of trying or intending. As interior, psychological activities, they automatically succeed. For the intentions
which build community seek the welfare of a beloved as their
ultimate end. That is, communal acts are acts of altruistic
love, and *vice versa*. In the deepest sense, then, sincere efforts to build community always succeed. To try to love is
to love. And to love is to establish the tie that binds. Good
intentions are, of their very nature, communal, and thus they
always establish community as the interior state of those who
hold them.

When one of our ancestors in the Olduvai Gorge tried his
best to find food and share it, but couldn't find any because it
just wasn't there, his interior achievement of community was
just as complete as if he had found the food. For community
is basically love, and when love is complete, community is,
too. But we have to make a careful distinction here. To
say that his failure to bring about the actual feeding that
he intended was no detriment to community is not to say
that outward actions and practical results count for nothing.
For a sincere intention leads to one's best efforts. Otherwise
it is not sincere. Altruism that doesn't urge us to our best
practical efforts is really masked self-primacy, and thus anti-

---

[32] The following view of the relations between communal actions and praxis is
based on Aquinas' view of the relations between interior and exterior acts, *S. Th.* I-II,
20, "On the Goodness and Malice of External Human Acts."

communal in both act and intention. Our friend, then, could not have said, "Well, I think I'll just rest today and let the others do the work. After all, I'll be with them in spirit." Laziness is a sure sign of egocentric intentions, and thus of a lack of the only motivation that can make community real. And finally, if one of these primitives had stockpiled food for himself only to find the others devouring it against his will, he would have no claim to community whatsoever. The practical effect would have been there, for the food would have been shared. But the sharing would not have been communal, even in some minimal way, for our hoarder. He was lacking the primary interior requirement for building community, the altruism which makes one's outward actions a means to the welfare of those he identifies as his other selves.

A communal person thus has to live something of a paradox in his efforts to integrate his interior attitudes with his outward actions, his intentions with his praxis. He has to have, as the minimum requirement for the realization of community, intentions that are sincerely altruistic. And those motives, carrying an implicit will to lay down his life for his friends, will lead him to make his best possible effort in the world of time and space. Then his intention, which leads to his best efforts, will realize community even if all practical results are frustrated. When we are frustrated in our praxis by any circumstances that are beyond our control, our best efforts are enough to bring about genuine community. We can achieve moral success in the midst of practical failure. And moral success is real success in the existential order of human love, even as it fails in the physical world of time and space. Moral victories are victories, indeed. One obvious contemporary example is the efforts of good-hearted people to bring about racial integration in some of our large cities. Acting with the best of intentions, their massive efforts over long periods of time have often left the races as separate as ever. Bussing thousands of school children has sometimes failed either to improve their education or to bring about greater racial harmony. And yet, we can say that these best efforts have brought about the full reality of community as an interior regime. Love always builds community, even when efforts to enflesh that love might fail. The only requirement is that love be sincere, so that the practical failures are not intended, even by default.

But this built-in success of communal intentions is no cause to be smug, or to make efforts that are less than our best. For when failures to achieve practical results are due to our own deliberate deficiencies, then the failures do indeed count. They count morally, which is to say, they inhibit our existential fulfillment. If my efforts are half-hearted, then my intentions are not truly altruistic. My ultimate end is, to some extent, at least, my own ease and comfort. And that egocentric motivation is always, and at once, the sure destruction of community. In fact, we can go even further. Practical results that come about by accident, and not because of our altruistic ends, give only the appearance of community, not its reality. If racial integration of schools were to come about without my intentions, for example, or even as an unintended result of my egocentric intentions, I would not thereby partake of community. I might associate with both blacks and whites, but I would not be in communion with them – or with anyone else, for that matter.

Thus the striving for community is a delicate process, requiring a synthesis between sincere motives and sincere efforts in outward actions. If we must choose between the two, then the motives are the more important, and sometimes the mere intention of community is enough to bring it about. Once we take community as an ultimate end, so that we then direct our praxis along lines which are the means to communal associations, then community instantly becomes real. There is comfort for the communal-minded in the premise that community desired is community achieved. But at the same time, a sincere desire for community leads us to do our personal best to bring it about in the practical realm. That demand for praxis will test the sincerity with which we intend the good of others as our ultimate end. If our ends are ultimately egocentric, we will not have the courage to make our best efforts, and then community will not become real in our praxis. And so, the practical demand is equally as severe as the intentional. For practical success counts for nothing morally, communally, without sincere altruistic motives. It is conceivable, then, that we might solve all of our horrendous social problems and still not achieve the reality of community. We might integrate the races, distribute the world's wealth with perfect equity, and disarm nations once and for all. But if we did all of that for egocentric motives, with our own use and pleasure as the ultimate end of that praxis, we would have a counterfeit of community that would leave us existentially alone.

In one sense, then, love is all we ever need to know. St. Augustine's maxim, "Love, and then do what you will," can serve as a perfect norm for all of our deliberate actions. It

can tell us what is communal and thus morally, humanly
right, and what is anti-communal and thus morally, humanly
wrong. Love is the standard by which we can judge our political arrangements, our family life, our cultural and social de-
velopments, our educational systems, our health care, and all
of our other deliberate associations with each other. For these
associations are nothing more than persons in action, intending ultimate ends and choosing the means by which to enact
those ends in the practical realm. Moral issues and questions
are community issues and questions, and thus questions and
issues of altruistic love. Such love is the distinctively human
trait. It is the arena in which the drama of human existential fulfillment is acted out. But it is the only guide we need
because of its utterly practical implications. For to love is
to make one's very best effort toward the means to the end,
toward the praxis that makes community a physical reality
as well.

Since community, moral goodness, and our existential
fulfillment all coincide, we can now see the important second
sense in which love is the tie that binds. Primarily, it binds
us together ontologically, brings us to enjoy, as our common
good, the many acts of existence by which we are diverse
members of the community of being. But there is an important moral binding here as well. We are bound, in the sense
of being obliged, to love, to do what is morally right, to enact
community. In other words, community is not an option for
us. It is an obligation, a categorical moral obligation, one
that we cannot escape. Community is our basic moral absolute, not a matter of preference or a value that is relative to
time, place or circumstances. To appropriate the community
of being in altruistic love is not just advisable for us, something good and right and praiseworthy. It is something that
we ought to do no matter what, something that we simply
must, in all conditions, strive for. The basis for this binding
power is the fact of our existence in the community of being.

At first glance, community does seem to be an option,
one of several ways in which people might choose to live. It
seems that we put it to ourselves as an option, a conditional
or hypothetical obligation. Thus,

> "If I want my human fulfillment, I must live in com-
> munity. And if I want to live in community, I must
> perform these actions and not those, with these mo-
> tives and not those. But right now, I don't care
> about my human fulfillment. I would rather enjoy
> the pleasure I get from this adultery than to be hu-

manly fulfilled in being faithful to my spouse in altruistic love."

Of course we can say such words to ourselves, and we
can then act them out. We have a physical and psychological freedom to "be what we ain't." We can act against our
own nature as members of the community of being. Psychologically, in our intent, moral obligation can be suspended,
of course. We can make it hypothetical in our minds. Without that freedom, we could not do moral wrong. For to do
moral wrong requires us to refuse to love, to make our own
use or pleasure the ultimate end for which we act, to be
anti-communal in both praxis and intent. But there is a
self-deceit at the root of such hypotheses, and an existential
penalty which makes them internally contradictory. Since the
penalty for not loving is unavoidable, the obligation to love,
to be communal in both intent and praxis, is inescapable as
well. It is not, finally, an option, or a hypothetical obligation. It is what we must do – categorically. The reason for
the necessity of the moral "ought" is the "is," or fact, of the
community of being.

Morally right, or communal, actions are obligatory because they are means to an end that is obligatory. That is,
love and community are not simple "if-then" matters, so that
our obligation to love is hypothetical, relative to our preferences. It is not a matter of "If you would achieve community,
then love altruistically." In reality, the end is not optional,
and thus the means to it are not optional matters either.
The case is, rather, "Since you must exist communally, then
you must love." Community is the only mode in which we
can fully exist as persons. Thus, we either exist communally
or not at all. If we fail to build community, we incur an
unavoidable penalty: the loss of our own existential fulfillment as persons. When we fail to build community, when
that failure is due to our own free choice and free intention
of an egocentric end, we introduce an element of non-being
into our own metaphysical structure. Evil, anti-communal
actions have their ends, of course. Otherwise we wouldn't
do them. And those ends – some pleasure or utility for ourselves – do constitute a kind of satisfaction or fulfillment.
When I violate my promise to my spouse, and thus my love
for him, in an adulterous affair, I find many benefits in so
doing. Otherwise I wouldn't do it. But the benefit that I
do not find is my distinctively personal existence, expanded
through my appropriation of the community of being. The
adultery brings only egocentric benefits which reinforce my

ontological loneliness.

We violate the tie that binds us, that obligates us, to communal actions, then, at the penalty of our own loss of personal existence. When we fail to love, we exist less fully than we might, are less real than we might be. Despite their emotional and physical rewards, anti-communal actions negate our very existence as persons. We are free, of course, to do that. We are physically and psychologically able to negate our own being. But to do so is to contradict ourselves, to think and do nonsense, non-sense. When we say, "I prefer some other fulfillment to my existential fullness," we are deceiving ourselves into thinking that we can, somehow, be fulfilled without really existing. But really, one who does not exist cannot enjoy anything. Thus the pleasures and other satisfactions that we buy at the price of our ontological healing are illusory, indeed. In short, we are obliged, or bound, willy-nilly, to love altruistically because that is the only way in which we can be real. Love is the tie by which we are bound to certain actions without any "if's, and's, or but's."

Moral obligation, then, the tie that binds us to communal intentions and actions, is but one particular kind of ontological bond. Beings are bound to each other existentially in many different ways. Some are causes of others. Thus is the sun bound to plants in the process of photosynthesis. Some are parasitical on others, as ivy on a tree. Some have bonds of various relationships, such as parents and children. And all beings, as we have seen, are bound together in their participation in the omnipresent Creator. Altruistic love is one such ontological bond, the bond which ties persons together precisely as persons, when we transcend ourselves to appropriate the community of being. But it is a distinctive ontological bond, one typical of persons in our existential fulfillment as persons. Hence that particular tie, as a bond or obligation, receives the special title of *moral*. Moral goodness is, quite simply, human existence. Community binds us morally because it binds us existentially.

Since the obligation toward community as an ultimate end is categorical rather than hypothetical, the obligation toward certain actions as being morally right and good is categorical as well. Let's suppose, for example, that I could steal a large sum of money without getting caught. I could thus escape all legal penalty. To make the case as clear as possible, suppose I have a good motive and produce good consequences – I steal the money in order to pay for a crippled child's operation. Am I still obliged not to steal the money?

On communal premises, the answer is "Yes." My obligation not to steal is not derived from the legal sanctions attached to stealing. Nor does it depend on my intermediate ends, nor on the consequences of my stealing. It depends on the structure of the world as a community whose appropriation is my onto-logical fulfillment. The stealing is a violation of community. It is a refusal to love the person whose money I steal. And since a failure to love one is a failure to love all, that stealing prevents my appropriation of the community of being. By stealing, I thus diminish my own existence. I am acting un-der an illusion – a self-imposed illusion, but an illusion all the same – that it is somehow fulfilling for me to negate my own fulfillment. The existential penalty is unavoidable, and thus my obligation not to steal is unconditional, absolute, cate-gorical. Community is the tie that binds me to respect the property of others. Moral goodness, then, is nothing more – and nothing less – than our existential fulfillment in com-munity. By the same token, moral evil is nothing more, and nothing less, than our freely chosen failure to exist as fully as we might. Moral obligation is just our need for ontological fulfillment, our need to exist in community.

When I fail in love, then, I miss my human fulfillment, just as surely as I miss my destination when I choose not to follow the road map. It is absurd for me to say, "I choose to find my fulfillment in enjoying the fruits of my stealing, or my adultery," because I have, to some extent, diminished my very existence in intending an anti-communal end. To the extent that I diminish my existence, there is no "I" to enjoy anything. Moral judgments, then, or statements that certain actions are to be done because right and others avoided be-cause wrong, do not make an illicit transition from "is" to "ought," from fact to value. Moral prescriptions are but de-scriptions of a special kind. They state the facts of human existence, just as the laws of science state facts about other forms of existence. To say "A husband ought to be faithful to his wife" is fundamentally just as much a statement of fact as "A neutered male cat should eat food with a low ash content." The laws of biology tell us the way things are in the processes of physical life. The laws of morality tell us how things are in the realm of deliberate actions by human beings.

This equation between the moral good and the existen-tial fulfillment that is distinctive of human persons has strong implications for the doing of moral evil. One is that when we intend moral evil, even before we enact our intention in

the realm of space and time, we immediately exclude ourselves from the community of being. A morally evil act is
one which, by definition, has the self as its ultimate end.
Such egocentric intent is a refusal to accept one's communal
mode of being. As soon as we intend moral evil, then, we
exclude ourselves from community. Evil-doers may belong to
many groups and associations, of course. And those groups
and associations will be communities for their members of
morally good intent. But evil-doers exclude themselves from
all genuine community by the motivation which determines
their moral identity. Community and evil intent are simply
incompatible with each other because the tie that binds ontologically is the same as the tie that binds morally. Thus
community and moral evil are utterly incompatible with each
other.

Such a conclusion seems severe, for it makes every deliberate action the choice of one of two stark options, indeed. It
implies that a single evil action is enough to delete our ontological fulfillment in community. It suggests that we cannot
do a single wrong action and still remain within any community. But these severe implications are clear when we understand the psychology of moral choice. In each deliberate
action, we orient ourselves, at least implicitly, to one of two
incompatible ultimate ends. And in so doing, we do not simply decide upon a particular action here and now, somehow
detached from ourselves, over and done with when we have
performed it. Rather, we give our very selves an identity that
is the source of the action. And that identity persists long
after the act is done, perhaps even for the rest of our lives.
We determine our very selves, not just our activities, when
we act in a fully human, deliberate way. We give ourselves an
identity as either a communal or an anti-communal person.

Common human experience reveals this fact. When
someone deceives us, for example, or uses or takes advantage of us, we expect more of the same when we meet that
person again. We are wary, suspicious, perhaps even totally
cynical about his intentions. He has not just performed an
action, over and done with. He has shown what kind of person he is. And just as one experience of being mistreated
leads us to expect more of the same, one experience of being
loved altruistically leads us to trust. When we meet someone
who has treated us lovingly in the past, we expect more of
the same. We are surprised if we are treated badly. We will
even say, "Boy, did I get fooled. I didn't think he was that
kind of person." Actions are means to ends, and our ends

determine who we are, our moral identities.

These spontaneous tendencies to mistrust and to trust have deep roots in the psychology of deliberate actions. When I fix upon some good as an intended end of one of my actions, I establish a relation between myself and that good which did not exist before. What was previously a good becomes my good – good not just in itself, but in relation to me. But when I transform a good into a good of my own, I do not change the good. I establish the new relation by making a change in myself. That is, I determine myself to be the kind of person for whom this end is good. The point is clear in an old joke. A man met an attractive woman at a party, and asked her if she would go to bed with him just once for $10,000. She replied, "Yes." As he closed the bedroom door, he said, "You know, I really don't have $10,000. I just said that to get you up here. You are so beautiful that I couldn't resist. Would $10 be enough?" The woman drew herself up and said, haughtily, "What do you think I am?" To that, her companion replied, "Well, we already established that. I was just trying to find out the price."

Aristotle made the point succinctly in his analysis of the psychology of the man who steals in order to commit adultery.[33] The man is a thief, of course, but more profoundly, because the stealing is a means to the affair which is his end, he is an adulterer. If we had to put him into a moral category, we would classify him among adulterers rather than among thieves, because the adultery is his end. The stealing is only a means to that, willed because of that. If he didn't have an affair to finance, he wouldn't steal. If he could finance his affair in some other way, then he wouldn't steal, either. As he would put it to himself, when he decides on stealing as the means to his end, "I wish there were another way. I'm really not this kind of person." But he is, of course, another kind – an adulterer. If we imagine another man who does the same actions, stealing and adultery, but with his motive reversed, the point is even more clear. Our second man has an affair in order to have the opportunity to steal. He, too, is both thief and adulterer, but since his affair is the means and stealing is his end, he belongs in the category of thieves. As he carries out his adultery, he says to himself, "Gee, I'm not really one to cheat on my wife, but this is too good a chance for some

---

[33] Aristotle's view that one who steals in order to commit adultery is more adulterer than thief is argued in his *Nichomachean Ethics*, V, 2, 1130a 24-32.

easy money. I can't pass it up." His primary identity as a
moral agent is decided by his freely intended end, not by the
means to it. He is not really an adulterer, as the first man
is, even though he does, indeed, commit adultery. Just as we
can expect our first man to continue to be an adulterer even
when he no longer needs to steal, so we expect our second
man to steal even when he has no need of an affair to give
him the opportunity. That is the kind of person each one is.

As it happens in Aristotle's example, both stealing and
adultery are morally wrong, and so, whichever is means to
the other as end, both of these men have a profoundly evil,
which is to say, anti-communal, moral identity that is determined by their ultimate ends. In both cases, their motivation is egocentric. Neither loves the one whose property
he steals, and neither loves the spouse whose marriage he
violates. For both, the motivation – the ultimate end that
they are "really after" – is some utility or pleasure (or both)
for themselves. And so, the primary or ultimate moral iden
tity of each is "violator of community," or "reinforcer of his
own ontological loneliness." They both may associate very
closely with other people, their partners in crime as well as
others. They may belong to many groupings in which they
act benevolently toward their fellows and form fairly stable,
civil, polite, enjoyable associations. Those associations may
even be genuinely communal for some or all of their other
members. But for evil-doers, associations are just that, as
sociations that are counterfeits of community. An evil-doer,
by that very fact, excludes himself from any appropriation of
the community of being.

Since our only entry into community is altruistic love,
community is a unique kind of good, at once psychological,
ontological, and moral. It is known and willed, thus psychological. It extends our existence, and is thus ontological. And
it perfects us precisely as persons, with the perfection that
is distinctive of human beings. This last aspect makes it our
moral good. It follows, then, that there can be no such reality as an evil community, a whole community of evil-doers.
Those who intend moral evil can, of course, collaborate in
very intricate and efficient ways to carry out the evil intentions that they all hold. They can form associations that
are quite remarkable as groups of human beings unified in a
common project. The Brinks robbers come to mind, as does
the Third Reich. Their evil intent, though, while seemingly
common to them all, was not. Each centered his will on the
private self to which he gave primacy, as his ultimate end.

Thus these groups had no ontological bond. They could only be collectivities, not genuine communities. They were fragmented in their being because their wills were, despite their agreements on intermediate ends and means, fragmented by their ultimate egocentric motives.

The Nazis, then, had only the apparent unity of a well-oiled machine. They did not, and could not have, shared any common ontological good. For such sharing requires altruistic love, love for all. And the psychological- ontological-moral solitude of the Nazis was a fact in spite of any concern that they might have had for their families and even for each other. We can believe that some of them were quite decent human beings in many respects, that they cared about the future of their Aryan society and aided each other's careers with a certain benevolence, even felt affection for their wives and children. But these superficial or intermediate good intentions were vitiated by their willingness to murder Jews and their other victims. To intend the murder of anyone is an inherent contradiction of the altruism which alone brings us into community. The logic of love, rooted in the community of being, has already led us to the conclusion that to love one is to love all, and to fail to love any one is to fail to love all. It now leads to the further conclusion that moral evil has no place whatsoever in community, that evil members of a community, and whole communities of evil-doers contradict the love which is the only tie that binds.

These results imply many ironies, not the least of which can be seen in the Holocaust. Paradoxically, some, perhaps even all of its victims could well have been in community with their oppressors. All they needed was an altruistic love (a love which, of course, wished them to give up their murderous ends). But their oppressors could not have been in community with anyone – not with their victims, and not even with each other. A community of evil-doers, an evil community, is a contradiction in terms. Evil collectivities can and do exist. Their members have, of course, the physical unity that all beings share, existing as they do by the omnipresence of the Creator. There is a certain goodness to that. But it is not the goodness that is distinctively human, the moral good. Evil-doers are evil, lacking existence, precisely as persons. A single evil intention is enough to destroy that psychological-ontological-moral entity known as community, for each and every individual who harbors such an intention.

CHAPTER VII
COMMUNITY AND LAW

Our need to return to the analysis of sincerity and to spell out the limits of its content has now become urgent. A blanket condemnation of all who willingly collaborated with the Third Reich seems harsh, indeed. And yet, that conclusion is the logical outcome of our argument thus far. For anyone's evil intent precludes his appropriation of the community of being. But an even harsher conclusion lurks in the shadows. It seems that a blanket condemnation of all social contracts, of all human associations that are in any way selective or conditional, is just as plausible. For both contractarians and evil-doers have been shown to have ultimately egocentric motives. And such motives make all the actions governed by those motives morally wrong. Those motives also make all the associations of those who harbor them anti-communal, mere associations that are counterfeits of genuine community. A new question arises, then, about sincerity. If sincerity is the rock-bottom, minimal requirement for anyone to come into community, what about those Nazis who sincerely believed in Aryan supremacy at any cost? What about those whose sincere view of human relationships is contractarian rather than communal? It would seem that sincerity has some limits that must be spelled out. Otherwise, literally anything would be permitted in human associations, including the Holocaust. Furthermore, it is evident that many contractarians are well-meaning, good-hearted, kind people who wish to live in peace with their fellows. In fact, an ardent devotion to justice is, in many instances, the hallmark of contractarian thought. Can such a search for justice be sincere, and thus fundamentally communal?

We have reached the point, then, where the content of sincere convictions must be spelled out. If to love is to will a good to someone, we need to know more specifically what the good is that a lover must will to his beloved. Candy is good, in a sense, and yet it would not be a loving parent who would give candy to a diabetic child. The good cannot simply be equated with what the beloved wants. Nor can it be simply equated with what the lover wants the beloved to have. We've all been victims, in one way or another, of someone who, with the best of intentions, insisted that we have, or do, something "for our own good," when really what was good for us was just to be left alone. To put the question

in moral terms, our entry into community comes in only one
way: by our freely intending the moral good as an ultimate
end. But what is the moral good that we must intend? It is
not any and all goods that can qualify. Which ones do, then?
And how are we to know them? Can we at least show that
some ends and purposes are so grossly wrong, so evidently
and universally evil, that no one could sincerely intend them
as altruistic ultimate ends? Can we specify others that are
so obviously right that no one could sincerely be mistaken
about them, so that all would be obligated to intend them?
The question is one of absolute or universal moral norms or
values.

     To discern such moral goods, and their opposite evils, is
no easy task. It is, fundamentally, the task of formulating
basic moral principles and then, in civilized communities, at
least, of using these as guidelines to the making of law. For
law, too, is a tie that binds. Our word *law* and those related
to it – *legislation, legal,* even *obligation* itself – come from
a Latin root that means "to bind," originally "to tie up an
animal so that it cannot stray." Law binds us to act in certain
ways and to refrain from acting in others. It is, at bottom, a
set of guidelines for our altruistic loving. Laws are statements
which tell us, more or less specifically, what goods we are
bound to wish to a beloved if we are to be bound to him
existentially, in community. Since our distinctively human,
moral goods are of two kinds, laws are of two kinds as well.
Some are universal, statements of what is good for each and
every human person simply as a human person. These are the
basic principles of morality. But individuals vary a great deal,
even to the point of a glorious uniqueness. Hence we also need
guidelines that are more specific, laws that state what is good
for only some individuals. There are no conflicts between
these, because for all the uniqueness of individuals, we are
all *homines sapientes.* Hence, whatever our individual goods
might be, they are not opposed to the universal human goods,
but are specific instances of them. All need medical care, for
example, but not all need orthopedic surgery. Moreover, not
all who need orthopedic surgery need arthroscopy on their
left knee to remove cartilage damaged in a football game.
But arthroscopy is part of, not opposed to, medical care.[34]

---

[34] This analysis, which interprets the basic and common precepts of law as guidelines for the love that generates community, is an interpretation of Aquinas' justly
famous treatise on law, especially *S. Th.* I-II, 94, 2, "Whether the Natural Law
Contains Several Precepts, or Only One?" This text, in concluding that natural law
contains several precepts which are unified by their common origin, indicates the way
in which basic moral principles come to be known – through reflection on the common

In small societies with a relatively simply mode of life, the discovering and formulating of these basic goods can be informal and unstructured. Leakey's food-sharers knew from their ordinary experience that food is a basic good for everyone. They may even have realized that the socializing that marks human feeding is a basic human good, too. These rudimentary institutions did not require any elaborate dialogue, and they were expressed in simple, prelinguistic gestures. These first humans had no need to organize themselves socially and politically, to set up a government and formulate a code of laws. The day did come, however, when political order, and law-making as part of it, became necessary. But whoever the first lawmakers were, their legislative process was not different in kind from the unspoken judgments of the first humans that it was good for them to share the food that they found. Law is law, that is, binding, because it is a judgment of what is necessary for human community. Law commands certain actions, and forbids others, depending on whether they are means to community or steps away from it. Law is prescriptive in saying what its subjects must do. But it is so because it is first descriptive, stating the means to becoming what we are in fact – members of a natural community with the potential to make that community our own by deliberate choice.

Law, then, is a set of guidelines to altruistic love. Given that ultimate end, laws guide our deliberations about the means to community. The laws of various political units may vary a great deal, and laws of the same polity may change somewhat as time goes by. But there is a constant norm for all laws, of all times and all places. The members of any group, any social or political unit, are first members of the human species. As such, all have a common ultimate end or purpose: appropriation of the community of being in altruistic love. Thus all the laws made by men have a common norm. That norm is a set of higher laws, the more basic and general laws which guide the building of community. A nation must first be a community, if it is to humanly fulfill its members. Its laws, then, must be guidelines to community for that particular segment of the human race. They must be nothing more, and nothing less, than specific statements of the goods to be wished to each other, by their subjects, in altruistic love. The actions which are prescribed as means

---

needs of human beings, the basic goods of human nature.

to community in any particular society must be specific instances of more general types of actions which are the means
to community for all human beings of all times and all places.
Laws thus guide, or direct us, in the same fashion as does a
road map. They tell us which path to follow, which outward
actions to take, in order to reach our human fulfillment in
community.

Laws, then, share the obligatory force of the end to which
they guide us. As we have seen, the obligation to seek community is not a hypothetical one, but categorical. It carries
an unavoidable sanction. For the penalty of failing to build
community is the diminution of our very existence as persons. Laws, too, have their obligatory power, and it is just
as categorical. Of course, the laws that men make also have
man-made sanctions attached to them. The penalties for violating them are fines, jail sentences, and so on. And these
sanctions give laws some of their binding power. In a sense,
we are obligated, or bound, to observe the traffic laws because
we will go to jail if we don't. The sheer physical power of the
law enforcement system is at the root of the binding power
of the law. But that physical obligation, that binding force,
is rooted in a deeper, existential one. Laws which are true
laws, and which thus have their full obligatory power, bind
us because they state the way to community. Their penalty,
then, or sanction, is the loss of community. And with the
loss of community comes a loss of our very existence as persons. Laws thus carry the same ultimate sanction, and have
the same categorical binding power, as does the community
which is their ultimate end. The binding power of law is
finally rooted in our need to heal our ontological loneliness.

We must stop at red lights, then, if we do not wish to
pay a fine or go to jail. But even if we could avoid those man-
made sanctions, we ought to stop at red lights, must stop at
red lights, lest we contradict what we are by what we do. We
disobey the law at the price of our own existential loss. In
his famous "Letter from the Birmingham Jail," Dr. Martin
Luther King., Jr., spoke to those who resisted civil rights legislation on the grounds that law cannot change men's hearts.
Dr. King agreed that it could not, but went on to say that it
could protect innocent people from those who have no hearts.
That protection comes about through the physical power of
the police and the courts. But law enforcement alone, while
it can establish an outward peace and order, cannot generate
community. Men's hearts must be changed if community is
to be real. Hence, one of the reasons for law enforcement is

a profoundly educational one. In attaching sanctions to our laws, we hope that, by constraining the outward behavior of those with anti-communal intentions, we will eventually convert them to altruism. Law, in other words, seeks to make men good, not just in the outward actions which they take as means to their various ends, but in the inward intentions of those ends also. For it is only in right intentions that community comes to be real.

This binding power of law, rooted as it is in our need to love altruistically so as to appropriate the community of being, gives some clues as to the nature of authority. Those who makes laws – and in a democracy, that is all of the adult citizens – need to meet certain qualifications. They must, of course, have the physical power to enforce the law. Quite apart from knowing and guiding our inward intentions, lawmakers must be able to coerce outward behavior, to protect the innocent from those who have no hearts. But that power can only be legitimate if it is rooted in something deeper. If it is not, might will make right, and the actions of the police will be unloving and thus anti-communal. In seeking the nature of authority, and the qualifications of law-makers, we can find a clue in the history of language. The term *authority* has two quite distinct meanings in our dictionary, meanings which indicate a shift from communal to contractual thinking among the speakers of English. We noted earlier a similar shift in the meanings of such terms as *kind, human, gentle* and *courteous*. In its earliest usage, with a meaning derived from a Latin term meaning "to augment or increase" *authority* meant one who originated new ideas and theories, or who made discoveries that augmented a field of knowledge. An authority was an expert, someone who knew things that other people did not know. We use the term in that meaning today, when we speak of someone's being an authority on Shakespeare, on the history of the Industrial Revolution, or on nuclear energy. But in modern times, another meaning has come to be primary in English usage, namely, authority as power. In this sense, now the more usual one, an authority is one who can control the behavior of others. An authority is one who has power – in the last analysis, physical power, through the agencies of law enforcement – to coerce the outward behavior of others.

Two different views of the law-maker correspond to these two different notions of authority. In the latter, contractual sense now prevalent in the English-speaking world, a law-maker is one who has access to power. The ones who formulate the guidelines to the actions of others are those who can command superior physical forces. And laws can be, as far as their content is concerned, whatever the law-makers can enforce. Might makes right. But in the older, communal sense, sanctions rooted in the law-makers' superior physical power are legitimate only as a tool of one who is an authority in the sense of expertise. An authority, a law-maker, must be qualified for that role by his knowledge. And the knowledge he must have, his expertise, if you will, must be precisely in the areas of human love and the community which love can generate. The power to enforce the law must be grounded in knowledge, in the expertise about the existential sanction of our nature as communal beings. Authority as power must be rooted in authority as knowledge. The qualified law-makers, then, are those who know what kind of behavior is conducive to community and what is not. Since, in a democracy – government of the people, by the people, and for the people – all the citizens are law-makers, then all the citizens must be knowledgeable in the ways of love. Community should be everyone's area of expertise.

The process of making law is modeled on the process of deliberation that we looked at earlier. Indeed, acts of legislating are but one instance of the many kinds of deliberate actions in which we either build community or lose it. The legislative process, then, is a process of formulating statements that certain behaviors – driving at a certain speed, for example – are ways of enacting altruistic love, and others are the opposite. Once such prescriptive statements are formulated, they are at once binding categorically because they are grounded in our existential need to seek community. But a society that has both actual and potential members who resist and destroy community needs protection from them. And so other sanctions are attached, so as to coerce the outward behavior of those with evil intentions. With the establishment of the law-enforcement arm, the law-makers' task is done. But throughout the law-making and law-enforcement process, those who make the laws are able to say how we should behave because of their superior understanding of what we are. Authority as power has its ground in authority as knowledge.

But what, exactly, do law-makers need to know? Like any other communal persons, they must be sincere in their convictions about right and wrong behavior. But, as we have seen, there are some limits to sincerity. Laws cannot be formulated to require just any behavior whatsoever. The

Nuremberg trials put such relativism to rest once and for all. There is, then, a definite content to the expert knowledge that law-makers must claim, the content of the convictions of any sincere person. And yet, such expertise is not easy to come by. Obviously, a law-maker, as any sincere person, must know the basic goods that are due to all human beings as members of the species *homo sapiens*. Any lover must wish certain basic goods to any beloved. What those goods are is determined by the common humanity of both. Thus certain values, or goods, certain behaviors, ought to be common to primitive and civilized peoples, to agricultural and industrial societies, to monarchies and democracies, to eastern and western cultures, to old and young, men and women, and so on. If we do have a common human nature, then we are under some common prescriptions as to our behavior. And those common prescriptions ought to show up in the laws of all societies.

Anthropologists have found that there are, indeed, certain basic values in the laws of all known societies.[35] There are some basic moral principles that are used as norms for law-making by men of all times and places. If we examine these basic values in the light of community, we can see why they should appear so widely. They correspond exactly to needs that are common to all human persons, to goods that any lover must wish to any beloved. They thus specify what we must do in terms of what we are. They show certain actions to be absolutely obligatory as conditions for our fully flourishing existence as human persons. In fact, we will be able to see that community, and indeed, human survival, would not be possible if these basic values were to be systematically violated. They are at least five in number: the protection of human life, the regulation of sexual behavior, the nurture of children, respect for property, and opportunity to search for truth. These five values have been, and rightly so, guidelines for law-makers everywhere. They are absolute necessities for the existence of community. In fact, the process of making law could fairly be described as a process of making these general values specific to a particular society or nation. They constitute the minimal content of a sincere person's convictions. No one who deliberately refused any

---

[35] For a survey of anthropological evidence that there are, indeed, several basic moral principles (strikingly similar to those suggested by Aquinas in *S. Th.*, I-II, 94, 2), principles common to all known human societies, see Thomas E. Davitt, *The Basic Values in Law* (Milwaukee, Marquette University Press, 1978).

one of them to any single person could be an altruistic lover
who might appropriate the community of being.

These basic values take different forms in different societies, as we would expect. Thus, the protection of human
life is legislated differently in primitive and in civilized societies. But wherever human beings have been found, with
either written or unwritten laws, the taking of human life has
been restricted more narrowly than the taking of the lives of
other animals. Some laws allow killing outside the tribe but
not within it. Some allow killing in revenge, others only in
self-defense, and so on. But no known society has ever legislated, or approved of, the wanton taking of human life. These
restrictions on the killing of human persons, varied though
they are, all rest on a recognition of fellowship. They reflect
the identification which is at the heart of the most rudimentary altruistic love. For in protecting another's life, we wish
him his continuing existence. The mere existence of at least
some members of our species is recognized everywhere as a
basic human good, a norm for human actions and for the
laws that regulate those. Without the existence of our fellows, community would not be possible. Without wishing to
them their physical existence, we cannot claim to love them.

Some regulation of sexual activities is a second universal
moral and legal prescription. Of course, there is a bewildering and fascinating variety in the customs and laws pertaining
to human sexuality. But what is noteworthy here is that no
known society has ever valued complete sexual promiscuity
or held it as a norm for human behavior. Restrictions may
vary, but there are always some, such as a ban on rape or
incest. These universal regulations of sexual activities reveal
some special importance in these actions compared to other
actions that are not similarly restricted. Sexual intercourse
has a higher value among humans than among the other animals, where utter promiscuity may be the norm. And sexual
intercourse has a higher value among humans than do other
human actions. There is something about it that prevents
a totally casual attitude. That something is, of course, the
power of sexual intercourse to express either altruistic love
or egocentric manipulation. No other action that we humans
engage in has the same psychological power. Its value as a
way to community, and its potential to destroy community,
cannot be overestimated. Because of such power, sexual actions need restraint. No one who was utterly promiscuous
sexually could claim to love altruistically.

The children who result from sexual union are also given a universal value in various human societies. Once again, the general value is made specific in myriad customs and laws. The ways of caring for children and educating them to take their place in adult society are enormously complex and varied. But all known societies have some requirements for taking care of children and educating them. Some have approved of exposing unwanted children and aborting unwanted fetuses. But no society has ever held up as an ideal, as a norm for behavior reflected in its laws and customs, the total neglect of children or an utter disregard for their education. Children are universally recognized as having a value superior to that of other animals and of material objects. In that recognition, once again, we see the rudiments of identification. Even those members of our species who are totally unable to return our love and care, the helpless ones who serve no useful social purpose, are treasured and loved for their own sakes. One who would be totally indifferent to the nurturing of children could hardly claim to love anyone altruistically.

Property is a fourth universal human value. Wherever we find human beings living together, we find regulations about which material things belong to whom. Ownership is recognized and respected. Not just anyone can consume just any food, wear just any clothes, use just any tools or weapons, or occupy just any space. Material things cannot be used and occupied by several people at once, and those that are consumed in the using cannot even be shared. Property laws, like all others, vary a great deal from one situation to another. But there has never been a society, no matter how simple and few its possessions, that recommended indifference to ownership. What is one person's cannot simultaneously be another's, and without owning some things, we cannot survive. Property, then, is essential to community. No one can love another without wishing him to have food, clothing, shelter and space that are his and his alone.

The inquiry into truth is a fifth value that is treasured and protected by the laws of every known society. The freedom to search for truth, the obligation to tell the truth, the right to know, the duty to discover and honestly communicate truth — all these components of inquiry are also universal human values. The regulations that govern discovery and communication differ from culture to culture. But there has never been found a group of human persons who had as their norm an utter indifference to knowledge about them-

selves, about each other, and about the world. Deceit and
ignorance are nowhere valued as standard behaviors. The
connections between curiosity and community, and between
honest communication and community are evident enough.
At the very least, we need to know who is a candidate for
our love and who isn't. We need to distinguish those of our
kind from other beings in order to identify with them. But
once we know which beings are our fellows and which are not,
we also need to know their inner selves. One important segment of the truth about the world is the truth about the inner
worlds of our fellow humans. And that truth is not accessible
unless it be told. Honest communication, then, is an absolute prerequisite for identification, and thus for the altruistic
love that builds community. Various societies tolerate some
kinds and degrees of deception, secrecy, intellectual laziness
and ignorance. But none has ever lived, and none ever could
live, under a norm of complete indifference to truth.

These five basic values, found in the laws of all known
societies, are absolutely necessary guides to the outward behavior of anyone whose intent toward his fellows is altruistic.
They are, then, the building blocks of community, sanctioned
by the only kind of existence we can have — communal. In
order to see how crucial they are, we need only try to imagine
an individual or an association that did not make a sincere
effort to follow these prescriptions. What would an individual person be like who was completely indifferent to the
protection of human life, his own and that of his fellows?
He would not eat or sleep, seek shelter from the elements
or desire health care. He would be indifferent to accidental
dangers to his life and health, as well as to the lives and the
health of his fellows. He would regularly imperil the sheer
physical existence, safety and comfort that are the basic prerequisites to love and community. Suppose, further, that this
fellow was completely casual about his sexual behavior, copulating (and allowing others to copulate with him) entirely
at whim – whenever, wherever, however, and with whomever
impulses would lead. Imagine him utterly devoid of concern
for the welfare of children, his own and others, allowing them
to fend for themselves from the moment of birth. To continue the hypothesis, let this man have no regard for property, using and consuming for his own benefit whatever came
to hand. Finally, picture him devoid of all curiosity about
anything, the weather as well as the thoughts and feelings of
those around him, babbling nonsense and deceit instead of
trying to honestly communicate. Such a person would be, by

anyone's standards, abnormal – either profoundly retarded or mentally ill. He would not, indeed, survive very long, even as an isolated individual. But what he would be lacking is precisely the communal tendency that is natural to, and thus normative of, human behavior. The person we have described would be egocentric in the extreme.

If we try to imagine an entire society of such individuals, the communal tendency of human beings becomes even more evident. What would a group be like who were completely careless of each other's lives? They would neglect health and safety, both their own and each other's. They would kill each other as casually as they might swat mosquitoes or step on ants. Their sexual actions would be entirely wanton, with rape, incest and child abuse the order of the day. Their children would be unfed, exposed, assigned to no family relationships, given no instruction in how to live. No one would have any regard for what belonged to whom, as each ate whatever food came to hand, used whatever clothes, tools, weapons, space and housing his physical strength could command. No one would converse about anything, as all curiosity would be suppressed and laziness and deception would mark their interchanges. We need only describe such a society in order to proscribe it. No such society could exist, let alone thrive and develop.

These basic values common to all laws are, then, no accident. They are prescriptive because they are first descriptive. They state what, as a matter of fact, members of our species ought to do in order to exist and thrive, just as the laws of any other species – maple trees, say – state the behaviors that enable their members to exist and thrive. Our communal impulse is the root of the binding power of our laws. Ought is thus rooted in is, and does not need to be derived from it by elaborate or arcane philosophical arguments. Because they are so universally evident as to appear in the laws of all known societies, we can count at least these five basic values as the minimal content of the convictions of any sincere mind. The devotion to Truth requires that everyone adhere to these specific truths. They are accessible to any sane adult of normal intelligence, and thus cannot be sincerely denied. Anyone who would deny them would be incapable of community – retarded, mentally ill, a hypocrite or a fanatic. And so, these basic moral values constitute a touchstone of sincerity. Anyone who would love altruistically must recognize, in his intentions and in his actions, the goodness of human life and sexuality, of children and of property, and of truth

itself. These are the goods which he must wish to others, for
their sakes, in the altruistic love by which we appropriate the
community of being.

A negative judgment on the Nazis, then, is not too harsh.
Their defense — that they were obeying the laws of the
land — was rejected by the Nuremberg judges, and they
were tried, convicted and punished for perpetrating "crimes
against humanity." Ignorance was no excuse. The laws of a
body politic that contradict the first of our five basic values,
recommending wanton slaying of other human beings, do not
bind, for they are not true laws. Any normal adult can recognize the evil of the Holocaust, and so, those who claimed
not to do so could be judged insincere. They were rightly
held instead to what the basic moral values bind all of us to,
namely, respect for innocent life.

Social contract theory, though, and social contract practice, would seem to be a different question. Gross immorality
is not their hallmark. Indeed, a strong concern for liberty and
justice and for human rights, for duties that respect others'
rights, constitute important ideals not just for adherents to
these philosophical theories, but also to people who routinely
form friendships based on usefulness and pleasure. Contracts,
indeed, can be seen as negotiations of rights and duties, with
justice as the norm of their negotiations. Various listings of
universal human rights, such as the *United Nations Declaration on Human Rights*, correspond rather closely to the five
basic values prescribed above. The rights to life and property,
the protection of the family, honesty in written and spoken
communication – all of these are honored by millions of people who live by a contractual model for friendship and society.
Are justice, rights and duties also part of the content which
we must accept as part of any sincere convictions about human behavior and human associations? Are these, in and of
themselves, communal, not just contractual, values?

Once again, the history of English usage offers us an
important clue. The term *just* is derived from the Latin word
for law, *jus*. But *justice* and its synonym *fairness* have had
two fundamentally different meanings in English usage. The
first, earlier and communal meaning refers to the objective
reality of the world. The just is that which has a basis in
fact, something which is true or accurate, as a just measure
that a carpenter might use. The primary meaning of *fair* is,
"beautiful, pleasing in itself, good according to the nature of
things rather than human contrivance." Justness and fairness
in moral matters, then, are characteristics of those deliberate

acts which conform to the way things are. Just and fair
actions are those which promote our natural communality.
Justice and fairness, as is the authority which regulates them,
are rooted in altruistic love. Laws are just and fair when
they reflect a correct knowledge of community and its ways,
knowledge that constitutes someone an authority with the
right to make laws. The scope of justice is thus the scope of
love, and that in turn is the scope of all deliberate actions
that are morally right, the scope of all distinctively human
life and fulfillment.

But in a social contract view, all the basic moral and
legal terms are changed. *Obligation, authority, justice, rights*
and *duties* — all of these are transformed when the basic
perspective changes from communal to contractual premises.
Atomic, detached individuals have no categorical obligation
to associate with each other at all. They do so for the sake of
their own utility and/or pleasure. And so, their obligations
to certain actions are hypothetical. Their contracts take the
form, "If you would obtain such-and-such a result, then you
must do such-and-such," "If you want to be an American,
then you must observe the income tax laws." But there is no
prior necessity to be an American. If taxes become too bur-
densome, I simply excuse myself from the obligation to pay
them. If it is more beneficial to be a Canadian or Swiss citizen, I move to Canada or Switzerland. In the final analysis all
my associations are contingent on the excess of benefits over
cost. Since no one has any inherent obligation to associate
with anyone else, when people do choose to associate, the
ties that bind them are conditional. The actions which are
called for by reason of their association, then, are conditional
as well.

There is no universal norm for human fulfillment that
serves as a norm for contractual associations. Each individual
defines his fulfillment for himself. Indeed, the term *personal*
fulfillment does not mean, as it does in communal thought,
fulfillment precisely as a person, and hence through the love
that is distinctive of persons. Rather, *personal* means "private, nobody's business but my own." Each person defines
his fulfillment as he sees fit, and associations, along with the
contracts which regulate them, come about only because one
individual seeking his personal fulfillment comes into conflict
with others seeking theirs. Contracts, moral values and laws
all originate as efforts to resolve conflicts of rights. Authorities are those with power rather than knowledge. The law-
makers are those who have access to enough physical force to

compel people's obedience. And the law-makers attach sanctions which have little or no intrinsic connection to the laws – fines, jail terms, and so on. There is no intrinsic connection between legal sanctions and personal fulfillment, just as there is none between personal fulfillment and the contract itself. The result is that anyone who can violate the law for his own benefit, and escape any sanction, ought to do so. Why not steal if I can do so with impunity, especially when I do it for some good reason, such as providing surgery to a crippled child?

A contract, then, serves as a norm for the behavior of its parties, but the way in which it serves as a norm is different from the way in which community is a norm for its members. For contractarians, the contract itself is a convention, and its purpose is the individual fulfillment, in terms of utility and pleasure, of those who accept it. It is a norm for deciding on right and wrong actions, then. But "morally right" does not mean "in conformity with what we are by nature as communal beings." It means "what we have agreed upon, and what we can thus change at will." Morally good actions are those that are acceptable to one's chosen society, according to the tacit or explicit contract on which the society rests. But there is no further norm by which the contract itself can be judged.

Justice may seem to be such a norm, but if we examine it, we see that it is not. Rather, the contract decides what is just, instead of justice deciding what is a morally right or good contract. The second meaning of justice in our dictionary, the contractual meaning that prevails in contemporary usage, is "fairness." *Fairness*, in its turn, is defined as impartiality. Contracts must be just, of course. They cannot be wholly arbitrary. The realm of justice, moreover, is in some sense the realm of morality. And so, parties to various social contracts are obliged, morally obliged, to be just and fair in their interactions with each other. But justice is not decided by an objective truth about human relations that is prior to all contracts. It has no reference to a natural communality and hence to obligations to love all in an altruistic love of each for each. Instead, justice requires us to treat all members of a given society impartially, not to play favorites or act out of any bias. A fair person balances competing claims. He negotiates, compromises, sees to it that both parties to a conflict receive equal benefits in return for equal costs.

When we look at justice and fairness as ways to community, however, they take on different content. What is just or fair is what conforms to facts. A just law, a just contract, a fair negotiation or settlement of a suit are all morally right because they reflect objective knowledge of our naturally communal existence. Just laws are formulated by authorities who have a correct, true knowledge of the world. But then, these laws are also just in the contractarian sense. They are fair, without bias, favoritism, or fraud, and they aim at a balancing of claims, of costs and benefits. They are fair in these secondary ways, however, only because they are already fair in the primary sense of beautiful, pleasing, and good according to the nature of things. Their justice or fairness is not contrived, but discovered in the community of being.

In both community and in contracts, then, law seeks to establish justice and fairness in our associations with each other. But the two modes of relating human persons to each other differ profoundly in their notions of what justice and fairness are, as well as in their notions of authority, obli gation, and law itself. For communal relations, justice and fairness, authority and obligation are rooted in love, the love which seeks the appropriation of the community of being. In contractual relations, these are all rooted in an egocentric self-primacy which precludes genuine community from the start. The same difference occurs in the notions of rights and duties – the rights which we can claim from each other, the duties by which we are obliged to respect and grant each other's rights. In a contractarian view, we demand our rights out of a position of power. We can make claims on each other. A claim is an authoritative demand of a right, on the basis of fairness. But fairness is a contrivance, a convention, and not the recognizing of a given state of affairs in the world which is prior to all contracts. Hence any claim is fundamentally artificial, too, and my success in making it will ultimately depend on my power to compel others to grant it.

Duties are similarly artificial, for they correspond to rights. One person's rights are another person's duties. A duty is a debt, something that is due, or owed, to another. But debts do not come about by any natural relations between persons. They result from contracts, and are thus contrived and artificial. Whether a right does impose a duty, then, whether the right in question is fit, proper, correct – in a word, fair – depends on the terms of the contract. Claims may be made in the name of justice, and justice may be called a moral norm, but morality retains its fundamentally conventional character. It is the association that decides

what is moral, rather than a prior morality deciding about
the rightness of a given association.[36]

The communal view of human associations retains the
older, once standard meaning of rights and duties. The term
right, derived from the Latin word meaning "straight," (*rectus*) is related to other terms that have the same root, such
as *correct* and *direct*. The Latin term referred primarily to
a straight line, as contrasted with a crooked, bent or curved
one. Rectitude, then, in its original sense, is the opposite of
deviation. To give someone direction is to give him information that is correct, to show him the right path, the one that
will take him straight to his destination. These spatial meanings underlie the older, communal usage of the term *right* in
its legal and moral senses. A right, thus, is something to
which one has a just claim. But a just claim is, first of all,
correct, and, because it is correct, it is fair in the sense of
beautiful – an element of a beautiful state of affairs. Rights,
in sum, are fundamental needs. They are just claims to what
we have to have in order to love altruistically and thereby appropriate the communality that is ours by nature. They are
the behaviors that we need, in ourselves and from others, in
order to find the straight path to our communal destination.
When, in a community context, we list human rights, then,
we are giving directions, indicating correctly those actions
which are the means to community, and other actions which
are deviations from it. Duties are our categorical obligations
to grant to others the rights which they justly claim.

It follows, then, that communal rights and duties are
entirely reciprocal, so that every right that one person has
imposes a corresponding duty on all others – not just those
who negotiate various contracts with him. Our obligation to
love requires us to wish to others, for their sakes, all that they
need in order to exercise their own loving appropriation of the
community of being. Their rights are, simply, those needs.
I may claim from all other human beings, then, whatever I
need in order to love altruistically. And my claim of those
needs imposes a categorical duty upon them. My basic rights,
and their basic duties, do not depend on the various associations that we negotiate with each other. Rather, the validity
of our associations depends on those rights and duties. An
association which deprives anyone of what he needs in order

---

[36] John Rawls' well-known *A Theory of Justice* (Cambrige: Harvard University
Press, 1971) offers an elaborate argument for a contractual view of justice.

to love, that is, of his human rights, is anti-communal. And since it is anti-communal, it violates everyone's prior categorical obligation to love. No such association can have any validity. None has any authority, nor any right to make laws or impose obligations, no right, indeed, to exist.

One man's rights, then, are another man's duties. When I justly claim one of my rights from another person, I am simply reminding him of what we both need to do in order to love, and thereby become what we already are – members of the community of being. I am not making an arbitrary claim whose validity depends on my power to enforce it. It follows that there can be no genuine conflicts of rights, as there might seem to be in contractual relationships. For when I claim one of my rights, thereby imposing on another a corresponding duty, I do so on the basis of our common humanity. Our common humanity has a common destiny, namely, community, and a common path to it. There is a set of actions that are the same for all human beings because they are the means to the end which is the same for all of us. Those actions constitute a common set of rights and duties. In fact, rights and duties are simply two different aspects of the same realities, of the needs which constitute our capacity to appropriate the community of being in altruistic love. Those needs are rights from the point of view of one who has them, and duties from the point of view of one who is to lovingly fulfill them. Since all of us have a categorical obligation to love, the set of rights corresponds perfectly to the set of duties, and these are basically the same for every member of the species *homo sapiens*. They are the five basic values found everywhere in law.

It follows, then, that there can be no genuine conflict of rights. There are genuine conflicts, of course, but these will always be conflicts between a genuine right and a spurious one. In simpler terms, there can be no genuine conflict between basic human needs. There is an important difference between needs and desires, between what we have to have in order to love and what we would like to have in order to enjoy life. The former are our rights, but the latter are not. Hence any apparent conflict between rights is just that – an apparent one. It is a conflict between a need and a desire, between a genuine right and a spurious one. Of course, such conflicts have to be negotiated and settled. But negotiation and settlement will not be a decision as to which of two rights takes priority over the other. A resolution will, instead, be the effort to discern which demand is a genuine right and which is a false claim, which is a need and which is a desire.

To take a current example, the abortion debate in the
United States is posed, by both sides, as a conflict of rights.
One side argues that the mother's rights to privacy and choice
take precedence over the fetus's right to life. The other side
argues the reverse, that the right to life is primary. Such
debates are typical of conflicts as they are negotiated on contractual terms. But in the light of communal principles, a
different approach is called for. A pregnant woman, as a human person, needs to love altruistically in order to remedy
her existential loneliness, and has an absolute right to whatever she needs for the exercise of such love. Her fetus, as at
least a potential if not actual human being, has the very same
need to love and absolute rights to whatever corresponds to
that need. Life is a prerequisite to the ability to love, and
hence both mother and child have absolute rights to life and
to whatever is necessary to support it. For the fetus, some
sort of gestation, natural or artificial, is necessary. For the
mother, conditions that make gestation and delivery safe are
her absolute right. But privacy, the ability to exercise individualistic liberty, is another matter. An alleged right to
privacy, in the sense of a right to make wholly isolated, arbitrary moral decisions, is a spurious one, a desire but not a
need. Certainly a woman, as a human person, has some sort
of a right to some sort of privacy, to freedom of conscience.
But that is not the privacy in question. As the slogan that
supports abortion on demand has it, she is claiming a right
to do whatever she wants with her own body. No such right
exists. Such privacy is not a need for the exercise of altruistic
love. This apparent conflict between rights, then, is between
a need that is a genuine right – that of the fetus to continuing
gestation and birth, and a desire – that of the mother to enjoy whatever utility or pleasure that a continuing pregnancy
and delivery might deprive her of. Not all abortion situations
are so simple, of course, as mere matters of convenience. But
many are, and they cannot be resolved, in communal terms,
by giving absolute priority to a supposed right to privacy as
arbitrary individual choice.

Once communal principles of morality are accepted, any
pregnancy is everybody's business. It is not so much a
woman's condition. It is that, of course. But more importantly, it is a baby's condition. The existence of babies,
however, from the moment of their conception, is a concern
of the entire community. The existence of its members, the
loss of some and the gaining of others, is a basic concern
of every member of any community. Thus questions as to

the continuing gestation and delivery of every fetus are the concerns of all in the community, not just the private terrain of pregnant women. But just as all have some say as to whether the baby's gestation shall continue, all have a duty to aid that gestation in whatever way they can. In a truly communal society, all adults love and care for all children, and for all other adults as well. This communal feature of a pregnancy, and thus of an abortion decision, does not mean, however, that the continuing life of the fetus always has an unquestioned priority over the mother's genuine needs. She has genuine needs, which constitute her rights as well. Thus if the mother's life is threatened by the pregnancy, then the life of the fetus is moot. For if she does not live, neither will the baby. Life-threatening pregnancies, then, allow for the removal of the threat. Abortion may be performed to save a mother's life.

But the justification of such abortions does not rest on a hierarchy of rights which give the mother's right to private choice a priority over her baby's right to life. Such a right to privacy is absurd on its face, for the right to life is fundamental to all others. Neither do we resolve this conflict by valuing her life over her baby's, as if we could compare two human lives and give one a higher value than the other. Rather, the resolution of a life-threatening pregnancy by removing the nonviable fetus is the discernment between a genuine right and a spurious one. The baby's right to life is no longer a genuine possibility because the baby's continuing development will kill the mother, and thus destroy the baby in the process. If the mother dies, the baby will, too. The baby's right to life is then spurious because it is not a real possibility. The only genuine right in the case, then, is the mother's right to life. But in other cases, where the mother's life were not threatened, the baby's right to life is a need that would take priority over the mother's desires for her own convenience, her comfort, and even, to some considerable extent, her health.

In conclusion, then, the five basic values in law are the same as universal moral principles. They describe, and prescribe, what everyone needs in order to appropriate the community of being in altruistic love. They are basic goods that anyone who would love must wish to his other self. They are also identical with genuine human rights and duties. They tell us what is just and fair in our dealings with each other. They spell out our categorical obligations to each other, and serve as norms for law-making. All of these are nothing more than formulations of what we all need in order to be what we already are: members of the community of being into which all sincere seekers of truth inquire. Whoever makes a sincere inquiry soon comes to see that every human person has a right not to be wantonly killed, and a duty to refrain from such killing. He sees that everyone has the right to sexual activity that bears the distinctively human quality of altruistic love, and everyone the duty to refrain from sexual activity that is not so intended. He sees that every child has a right to the care and education which will eventually enable him to love altruistically, and every adult the duty to provide such care and education for every child. He sees that each of us has a strict right to own those material goods that are necessary for our ability to love, and a corresponding duty to respect such ownership on the part of all other human persons. And he sees that every human person, old or young, primitive or civilized, rich or poor, male or female, has a right to seek and find the truth about the world, including especially the inner worlds of his fellow humans. He sees that every one of us has a corresponding duty to aid that search in the lives of our fellows. Finally, he sees that whatever desires may conflict with these rights and duties must give way to them, for the rights and duties, rooted in our communal way of existing, bear a categorical obligation. Their sanction is a justice that is fair, and a fairness that is existential. Law is law, that is, binding, because it tells us how to love. And that is what we must do in order to be what we are. Law's obligation is as categorical as the community of being in which it is rooted.

A sincere devotion to justice can save contractual relationships, then, and render them truly communal. But that sincerity, like any other, combines a willingness to die for what one sees to be true with a willingness to revise one's most cherished opinions in the light of objective evidence. In the case of a contractual devotion to justice and human rights, sincere devotees of these must be open to the implications of their sincerity. Would one give his life for justice, dying rather than violating one of the rights of his fellows? If so, he must ask himself why he would do so. The only rational basis on which to die for someone's rights is to seek justice as a reality, a concrete entity that is transcendent to us and can make demands on us. Justice is not one of our constructs, but something to which we submit ourselves. But a concrete, transcendent justice can only be one thing: the right, factual, beautiful state of affairs that precedes all our decisions and choices and governs them as their norm. And that is the community of being.

Any sincere devotee of justice and of human rights who accepts these implications of his own sincerity takes a giant step, then, toward accepting the premises on which community is based. He views the world as an order that he ought not to violate, which he ought to reduplicate in his intentions and his actions. He is on the way to recognizing that the worst sanction he can incur by violating justice and the rights of his fellows is his own separation from that right and beautiful order of things which is the community of being. Thus a sincere contractarian thirst for justice is already converting itself into the love by which we appropriate the community of being. In the final analysis, justice is fair (unbiased) because the world is fair (beautiful). Justice is a right (something which one might authoritatively claim) because it is right (in conformity with the way things are). A sincere devotion to justice is thus communal in its implicit assumptions, even as is a sincere inquiry into truth.

CHAPTER VIII

COMMUNITY AS A REAL IDEAL

The task of discerning universal moral norms, the precise goods that we must wish to someone that we love, is not finished by a listing of the basic and universal human goods that constitute everyone's rights and duties. Nor does the civil law, even when correctly expressive of those goods for a given polity, provide sufficient guidance. The basic values found in all laws, the basic needs of all human persons, as well as those of a body politic, are quite vague and general. "Respect human life," "Exercise sexual powers lovingly," "Care for children," "Respect property," and "Seek truth" are fine as far as they go. But as precepts of moral law, they are too vague and general to give us the guidance we need in real life. For there are no generic persons in the world, only concrete unique individuals. And there are no generic acts of love, either. Whenever I love, my inner intention and my outward action are so concrete, so tied to a particular person, a particular moment in time, a particular location in space, as to be unique and unrepeatable. If I am to appropriate the community of being in altruistic love, my respect for life, my loving sexuality, my concern for children, my respect for property and my search for truth have to be completely particularized. Otherwise my love is not real but a fantasy. It is Charlie Brown's attitude: "I love mankind It's people I can't stand."

But how, to take some concrete examples, am I to protect life when my teenager, flush with the excitement of passing his driver's test, wants to take the family car to a rock concert? How do I care for a child whose parents are verbally abusing it in public? How do I love a male colleague without either suppressing my sexual feelings or violating my marriage vows? How do I respect the property rights of the rich while I simultaneously care about the homeless and the starving? How do I honestly communicate my feelings without running off at the mouth in such a way that my companions cannot report theirs? Every deliberate action, every decision, is complex rather than simple, because every real situation is complex. And the more complex it is, the more difficult it is to know how to love in that situation.[37]

---

[37] The following model for moral decision-making is from Aquinas' discussions of the components of a human act (*S. Th.* I-II, 18 and 20), conscience (*S. Th.* I-II, 19),

In making moral – which is to say, community – decisions, our first step is to be clear about what it is that we propose to do, to define the essential core of our action. For example, many medical procedures, such as artificial life-support, seem at first glance to be life-saving procedures. But some are not. Giving oxygen to an anencephalic newborn, for example, is prolonging the agony of dying rather than saving a life. What appears to be stealing may not be – as when a starving person who cannot obtain food in any other way takes the surplus that a neighbor has accumulated. Knowing exactly what it is that we propose to do is not always easy. We must see the action, the physical action, in relation to the communal existence that is the constant fact of our lives. Thus, to take an example, sexual intercourse is not just the physical act of copulating, the same action performed by elephants, pigs, and all other mammals. It is the activity of persons in community. Consequently, whether they are married and to whom, whether they are blood relatives, whether both are consenting are facts central to what it is that they are doing. Adultery, incest and rape are different actions from each other, and different from marital sex, not just the same action performed in a variety of situations or circumstances.

But further, once having discerned what it is that we propose to do, we do have to look to the circumstances, to factors that are unique to each concrete situation. When and where we propose to do something, to whom and by what means, our own individual identity or role at the moment – all of these factors are part of the total reality of a concrete action, and thus part of what we intend and what we do. They are factors that partly determine whether an action is right or wrong, whether it builds or destroys community. The right action at the wrong time, or in the wrong place, will not be loving, but rather the reverse. For example, it is a good thing for a President of the United States to take off in his helicopter for some relaxation at Camp David. His doing so could well be the enactment of altruistic love for his fellow citizens. But the circumstance of time could be wrong. If he were to head for his helicopter while the red telephone was ringing, he would be violating our rights and refusing to appropriate the community of being. His relaxation in those circumstances would be wrong. A mother's

---

and the application of general moral principles to concrete actions (*S. Th.* I-II, 94, 4-6).

praying in church could be wrong if she had a sick child who needed her immediate attention. Perjury, always wrong for everyone, is worse when committed by an Attorney General. In many ways, circumstances can turn what would otherwise be a loving action into its opposite, or worsen an action that is evil to begin with. What is apt, by the very kind of action that it is, to build community can, in some circumstances, tear it down instead. Hence, there are important communal implications in Aristotle's famous statement that a good man not only does what is right, but also does it in the right place, at the right time, in the right way, and so on.

Other complexities arise when we think of the results of what we do. Looking to the future is uncertain at best, especially as our view becomes long range. Of course, every deliberate action has as its chief result, its end, the outcome or purpose which motivates us to perform the action. But most of our actions have many results, not just the one that motivates us. And some of these, those that are reasonably foreseeable, are included in the total action which we choose and act out. Bartenders are, in some states, held responsible for the people killed by customers who leave their taverns drunk, car keys in hand. To serve a drink to someone who is already intoxicated is not just to serve a drink. It is to become part of the future consequences of that serving. In an especially anguished decision, social workers in Minnesota recently lobbied for a law that would require unwed teenage mothers to take classes in the fundamentals of child care. To their surprise, the law was opposed by a pro-life activist group. Their fear was that the law would have evil consequences despite the good that was its intended end. The pro-life activists feared that some pregnant teenagers, faced with the prospect of compulsory classes in child-care, would opt to have abortions instead. Thus what we propose to do may seem loving, and all the circumstances apt, and yet community might be violated by a foreseeable consequence in the long range future.

Using community as a moral norm is, then, no easy matter, even when we specify its content in terms of the human rights and moral principles that make up the basic values found in all laws. The exact nature of what it is that we are doing is often murky to begin with. And that murkiness is complicated by the circumstances and consequences that we also have to take into account. One recent textbook in college ethics has a chapter entitled, "When Moral Choice is Ambiguous." Our understanding of community makes us wonder, "When is moral choice not ambiguous?" Indeed, the greatest ambiguity in any decision about our deliberate actions is one we have not yet looked at. And it is also the most important concern as far as community is concerned. That primary ambiguity has to do with the core reality of community, the altruistic love which is the tie that binds. Motivation, in other words, the subjective intention of the person who decides and acts in a certain way, at a particular time and place, with definite consequences, remains the key factor for the building of community. For if we do what is good, in a good situation, and with good consequences, but for self-serving motives, we vitiate an otherwise good action. Our own egoism, when it is the intended end of our actions, precludes community by the centering of our will on our own private good instead of that of another. T.S. Eliot's Becket put this stark moral fact well. He was tempted to return to Canterbury and face his martyrdom for the sake of his own vainglory, rather than serving his people in love. He saw himself doing the right thing, in the right circumstances, with several good consequences. But his heart was bad, and so, an otherwise communal deed would have been vitiated by an anti-communal intention. When he recognized his need to purify his heart, the saintly bishop said, "The last temptation is the greatest treason: To do the right deed for the wrong reason."[38]   Like any other community, the Church is destroyed when her members act out of egocentric motives. And human motives, of course, are always mixed, so that it is a wise man indeed who knows his own heart, his real reason for doing what he does.

We must never forget, then, that community is primarily a psychological state that is also moral and ontological. It is, in essence, the intending of a good to another, for that other's sake. An action might well be good, which is to say, apt to build community, in all of its other aspects, and still be wrong, or anti-communal, because of a self-serving motive on the part of the one who does it. It is seldom easy to achieve purity of intention, and it is never easy to know that we have. One test of our sincerity, though, is the price we are willing to pay in order to appropriate the community of being in altruistic love. If communal actions cost us significant money,

---

[38] These are the words of T. S. Eliot's Becket, in *Murder in The Cathedral*, as he considers the devil's temptation to seek martyrdom for the sake of personal glory. See T. S. Eliot and George Hoellering, *The Film of Murder in the Cathedral* (New York: Harcourt, Brace and Company, 1935), p. 63.

time, energy, or physical pain, and we carry them out anyway, we have a reliable sign of that purity of heart which is, as Kierkegaard put it, "to will one thing." On the other hand, altruistic actions that are highly beneficial to us should make us suspect our motives at once. Adolescent consciences that perceive an obligation to fornicate are not our most reliable guides to community.

A Chicago physician who recently made the news will serve as an example. He encloses with all his bills a statement that he considers his fees to be fair, but that patients who disagree may adjust them to suit their own ideas of fairness. When a reporter asked the doctor how many of his patients take advantage of that offer, he replied, "I don't know. I let my secretary handle all of that. I know that I have an adequate income, and that is all that I want to know. I am afraid that if I become too involved in money matters, I will lose my motivation for practicing medicine." This physician is, to say the least, unusual. But the system of setting medical fees in our country is an excellent case in point. It is certainly scandalous, from the point of view of community, that physicians as a class become wealthy, while poor people as a class lack the medical care that they need. It is hardly an exercise of altruistic love to profit financially from someone else's misfortunes. But decisions about medical fees are worth a careful look. They typify those in which community is either built or destroyed.

How might we decide fees in keeping with communal intentions on the part of doctors? A doctor needs, as the Chicago physician noted, an adequate income. But what is adequate? A general proposition would be that physicians need what all the rest of us need: adequate food, clothing, shelter, education, recreation, and financial security. These are the material needs of anyone who would wish to love altruistically, the basic rights of all human beings. Doctors need, as much as the rest of us, life and health, property and truth, opportunities to copulate lovingly and to nurture children. And it is certainly right and just, fair and in keeping with the beauty of the order of things, that physicians should be compensated for their skills, for their training and their labors. They certainly have a right to consider such circumstances as the cost of malpractice insurance and the ambiguities of long-range financial planning in their profession. But all of these genuine communal rights do not add up to a right to charge whatever the market will bear. They do not justify the policies of those who, for example, refuse to treat the poor or even to help patients fill out their insurance forms – policies which some physicians have been known to follow.

The setting of fees for medical services cannot follow a strict *quid pro quo* pricing policy, either. Physicians who would love altruistically cannot charge their patients what health is worth to them. Health is a pearl of great price. Indeed, it is beyond any price. Like the rest of the best things in life, it is priceless. There simply is no mathematical parity between health and money. We are left, then, with the physician's sincerity, and that of his patients, as the chief factor in setting his fees. One who sincerely loves his patients, who identifies them as his other selves, will make such love the basis of all his decisions, including those decisions that have to do with the fees he charges. And patients who sincerely love him will make that love the determining factor in their payments. Dare patients and physicians trust each other to show such love? At least one physician in Chicago seems to think so. Certainly without such trust a society will never be a genuine community.

In a physician's decision about his fees, we have, then, a model for all communal decision-making. Anyone who would love must think first of the intrinsic nature of the action he proposes to do. Some are intrinsically communal – seeking fair compensation for putting one's talents to the service of a needy client. Others – taking advantage of a victim of fate in order to maximize one's income – are not. Circumstances have to be considered, too. What time and place, what special facts of the persons involved create a situation in which an otherwise communal action might destroy community? A fee that is just for a wealthy patient might not be so for one who is poor. The far-reaching results are important, too. If an expensive, painful and risky procedure might restore a young person to a normal, healthy life, love might call for its performance. But if it will only prolong an agonized process of dying, love might demand that we leave well enough alone and let nature take her course. Last of all, and most important – in the rest of life as well as in medical ethics, "The last temptation is the greatest treason – to do the right deed for the wrong reason." Nothing builds community except altruistic love, the willing to another his good for his sake. And so the motive – the most difficult part of a human choice to assess – is also the most important of all. Do I love or not? Only when I do do I become who I am – a unique and irreplaceable member of the community of being.

When we put together these requirements for community, the chances of its coming to be seem slight, indeed. Such complexity multiplies our chances of going wrong. And purity of heart, the steady sincerity of altruistic motives, seems hopelessly visionary, indeed. When we put together all the requirements for community on a grand scale, such as a country, or the entire world, we must wonder indeed about the realism of such a hope. We might find, here and there, now and then, scattered individuals who manage an altruistic motive, as long as the price is not too high. And there will always be, we might hope, those rare individuals who become saints and martyrs. But it certainly seems Utopian to think that the masses of people might become unselfish in some sustained fashion, giving up all rivalries and living together in lasting peace and love. If community on such a global scale is not an adolescent fantasy, what is? One look at the slaughter bench of history, especially in our own century, ought to be enough for our sober disillusionment.

Such fears are not trivial. Any theory about human relationships has to have its plausibility tested against reality, against the reasonable expectations of real human beings. But even more is at stake here. We can easily make the best the enemy of the good. That is, by holding up to people ideals that are hopelessly high, we might discourage any and all efforts. And then our last state is worse than our first. The Utopian objection is not be be taken lightly. There are, however, two important answers to that objection, both of which have been briefly touched on several times through the course of our argument. If we can now bring these brief remarks together, we shall find some realistic hope for community, not only in the private lives of individuals, but on a grand, even global scale.

The first reply to the Utopian objection is a distinction between two kinds of ideals. The second is to show how moral success, of which community is an instance, differs from artistic success, how the road to hell is and is not paved with good intentions. The first kind of ideal is, indeed, Utopian. Ideals of this type are mere fantasies, visions and dreams that are impossible to achieve. Such ideals are the stuff of adolescent romance, sentimental illusions. The mental picture of a world in which most people were altruistic most of the time, doing the right deeds for the right reason, so that human relations were smooth and happy, social problems nonexistent, and international relations routinely peaceful is just such a fantasy. But an ideal can be of another kind, a fantasy that is not merely a fantasy, but a goal or purpose, an end in our deliberate actions. When we imagine a goal or purpose and intend to make it real, it both moves us to act and guides the ways in which we act. Such an ideal is, at first, a mental construct, a vision, a fantasy. But it is much more than that. It is a model of something that can become a reality. It is not just fantasized, but intended. Such an end does become real, thanks to the actions which it motivates and guides. Ideals of the second type are real ideals, ideals which can and sometimes do become real. They move us to act rather than not, and to act in one way rather than another. Community as such an ideal leads to actions which are the means of making it real.

The difference between these two types of ideals is the difference between a pitcher's fantasy that he is going to pitch a perfect game in every big league appearance and a real determination to win twenty games in a season while losing no more than ten or twelve. The pitcher with the first ideal is living in a dream world. The pitcher with the second ideal, however, may well find it becoming real. Community is an ideal of the second kind. Community is quite realizable. It can serve very well as a dream which can motivate and guide us toward making it a reality. Indeed, community is a special type of real ideal – a moral ideal. As such, its realization is achieved at the very moment that we make it our intended end. True, it leads us to speak words and to perform actions which fit that model in our minds, and to omit those that do not. But community becomes a reality from the first moment that it is intended, even before we begin to speak and act communally. In this one important feature, a moral ideal differs from other ideals, from those that may be called productive or artistic goals.[39] And here we see a second answer to the Utopian objection. In all of the arts, the quality of the product determines the success of the artist. If the work produced is defective, the artist is a failure. All the good intentions in the world cannot make him a success. He cannot ask for a prize on the grounds that he made his best effort. In a baseball game, or an art competition, no one can ask for credit – a winning score, or a blue ribbon – on the grounds that he tried. All that counts is performance, the production of a work that measures up in its concrete reality

---

[39] This distinction between moral and artistic success originates in Aristotle (*Nichomachean Ethics*, II, 4, 1105a17- 1105b18) and is developed by Aquinas in *S. Th.* I-II, 20.

to the intended model of what the work was meant to be. But in moral matters, the reverse is true. A man who tries his best to save a drowning child but fails because the current is too swift is just as much a hero as if he had actually saved the child. He gets credit for his good intentions. He deserves praise and gratitude for his best effort. He can plead tolerance and forgiveness for his failure. He can accept high honors for his heroism even though he doesn't succeed in the practical order.

Community is such a moral endeavor. It may, in a secondary way, also be artistic, issuing in a product, such as a family that is truly beautiful, or a nation with a noble unity. But such a product is not necessary for an effort toward community to be successful. Community begins to be real in the first moment that someone intends it, because the tie that binds is an intention. It is an altruistic love by which one wills to another his good for his sake. Such willing is accomplished interiorly, in a moment of time. Thus community becomes a reality even if the words and actions modeled on it ultimately fail in the world of time and space. People who sincerely intend community achieve it immediately. If they should then fail to establish associations that are outwardly as well as inwardly communal, they can still claim full credit for their good intentions. They can rightly be praised, not only for doing their best, but for actually achieving their moral goal. Their artistic failures can be tolerated and forgiven. The spouses in O. Henry's *Gift of the Magi* are an excellent example. With the best intentions in the world, the two willed to each other, through honest and unavoidable mistakes, Christmas gifts that were totally inappropriate and practically useless. But their practical failure did not detract one whit from the communion that their love brought them into. Even if they were to spend their entire married life in such blunders, they would be a great success as a couple. In fact, they would be more in communion with each other, and thus with the rest of the world, than another couple who always gave the right gifts, but did so with self-serving intentions. This latter couple would deserve no communal credit, no praise, no gratitude even if they achieved a spectacular external success. The closest outward unity we can imagine fails completely as community if it is the enactment of egocentric motives.

But lovers who mean well can claim credit for the real achievement of community, even when their best practical efforts fail. They do have the interior communion that is of the essence of anyone's appropriation of the community of being. Community, let us recall, is not a product of love. Community is love. But psychological community, the union of lover to beloved in intention, is ontological as well, even before it is acted out. That is, our success at building community, when we make our best effort to love but fail to externalize love in time and space, is a real success, not just a forgivable failure. When I intend some goal as my end or purpose, I already extend my very self outward to that end, making it my good. When that end is the well-being of someone I love altruistically, our psychological communion is already a moral, rather than an artistic, product. And in moral matters, the end is achieved at the very moment that it is intended. A desire to love is love already. An intention to will someone's fully flourishing existence is an act of willing it, and that willing is sufficient to bond the lover to his beloved.

Of course a sincere willing of my beloved's welfare leads to a second, further intention. That second act of intending is the artistic or practical one, the desire to do whatever my best efforts can achieve to bring about the practical state of affairs that my beloved's flourishing requires. But those best efforts may not be enough. Sometimes no practical action of any kind may be possible. At other times, none may be called for. Sometimes the best enactment of love is a simple, quiet, effortless enjoyment of what we already are together. Community can be fully real as a moral entity, then, without any external product of the intentions which constitute the tie that binds. An artistic failure can be a complete moral success. A moral victory may not be much comfort in an athletic contest, or any other artistic competition. But in matters of human relationships, moral victories are the best victories of all. The road to hell is paved by good intentions when those intentions are not sincere. But sincere intentions toward community inevitably pave the road to community itself.

A final answer to the Utopian objection is to consider the alternative. The alternative to a communal view of human life is some sort of contractual view, in which we associate with each other through selective, conditional and thus egocentric negotiations. In friendships based on desires for what is useful and/or pleasant for ourselves, practical or artistic success is the only kind that there is. To return to an earlier example, many of our big cities have seen massive, complex and expensive efforts to integrate the public schools through the compulsory busing of thousands of students. Both black

and white leaders are deciding, regretfully, that their efforts
have failed. Inner city schools remain increasingly segregated,
and black children are not even improving educationally as
their leaders had once hoped that they would. Our proposed
philosophy of community can find a profound moral consola-
tion in this artistic failure. We have achieved the reality of
community, at least those of us who have had sincere good
intentions, even if we haven't achieved genuine racial integration. But the Utopian objection is devastating to a contractual view of human associations. In this view, when a project
fails, the failure is total. There is no interior success to fall
back on. Contracts are conventions, agreements constructed
by those who take part in them for their own arbitrarily chosen and egocentric purposes. Thus there is no higher unity
by which an association can be judged a success. Its only criterion is in meeting its practical goals – the closeness in time
and space, the utility and pleasure for which the association
was built. Actions are right and good, just and fair, only if
they achieve a practical, external, artistic success. There is
no intention to achieve an inward, psychological communion
that is also ontological.

Thus, for contractarians, efforts to achieve unity through
some practical task, such as integrating the schools, have to
succeed outwardly. Otherwise the whole enterprise fails. The
intention to do something practical succeeds only if the some
thing practical gets done. And so, when people collaborate
not in a desire to be at one with each other interiorly – but to
build a common work of art, if they fail artistically, they fail
totally. Those who try and fail to integrate the schools have
no deeper unity that they can claim as a moral victory. For
they were not unified by a common purpose. Each was motivated by his own self-primacy, and their concerted outward
action was their only unity. In such projects, the failure to
achieve practical goals is a complete failure because practical
goals are the only ones they hold in common.

In community matters, then, practical failure can be a
success, and practical success can be a failure. For everything
depends on our purity of heart. The ideal of community becomes a reality as soon as someone takes it as his end, and
remains a reality as long as it remains his sincere intention.
Of course it is the hope of those who seek community that intentions will be acted out successfully in the realm of praxis.
World peace, intimate marriages and other friendships, integrated schools, a just distribution of the world's goods, the
total eradication of disease – all continue to call forth our

sincere best efforts. But meanwhile, as we strive for these practical realities, community itself is already real. It is real in the mind and heart of every individual person who tries to love altruistically. In the final analysis, then, a single well-intentioned person can establish and preserve the reality of community, without practical success, and even if no one returns his love. The tie that binds is our loving, not our being loved.

Hence we hold in our own hands the success or failure of our ontological fulfillment as communal persons. We ourselves decide whether or not to love. We ourselves determine our own intentions. Our inner appropriation of our communal being is impervious to all outside forces. Our highest ideal remains the praxis of altruistic love on as grand a scale as possible, the full practical reality of community. But failing that, we need not give up on community as a realizable ideal. Community is an interior regime which has its full reality in the heart of a single loving person. There was a logic, then, to Mother Theresa's Nobel Peace Prize, a logic that the Committee probably never suspected. For she does not merely help, in her small way, to bring about a more peaceful world. She is not just a model of what the rest of us need to be if we are to have a world at peace. Mother Theresa's achievement is much more extensive than that. For in the heart of Mother Theresa, thanks to her altruistic love, the whole world exists, and the world there is at peace. The world, at peace, is an in-heart reality whenever any one person sincerely and altruistically loves another, and thereby appropriates the entire community of being.

A final corollary is that the reality of community in the mind and heart of a single loving person offers a genuine hope for its outward extension, for love has a sacramental power. It is a symbol with the power to produce what it symbolizes. There is no guarantee, of course, for each person's decision to love is a free one. A communal person does not expect to be loved in return, nor does he demand reciprocity, gratitude or even recognition. But he hopes for these results, and his hope is not Utopian. It has a solid basis in reality. Love has certain psychological effects which constitute a kind of contagion. The process begins with the lover's own transformation. A communal person, already motivated by a devotion to the well-being of others, knows that the mere intention to build community is enough to make it real. He is quick, then, to give others credit for their good intentions. He is grateful for other people's efforts to love, even when those

efforts are misguided. He is ready to praise and thank his
associates, tolerant of their weaknesses and honest mistakes,
free of grudges against them.

But these attitudes are not sentimental, not a form of
romantic oversight. He is simply recognizing the communal identities of his fellows, in an entirely realistic way. He
identifies with them as individuals who are members of the
community of being before they even begin to return love for
love. And this dynamic of human love makes it highly conta-
gious. A lover is a credible person himself, and he makes love
credible to his fellows. For in the final analysis, we do not
come to believe in the reality of such interior states as love
and community through syllogisms and theories. We find
love real, and take community as a real ideal, through knowing people who make love credible because they themselves
are credible people.

We recognize in those who love us without ulterior motives the attitudes which psychologists have set forth as the
building blocks of adult, healthy intimacy. The foundation of
anyone's ability to love is a secure self-esteem that allows him
to abandon himself in intimate, game-free personal relationships. But such self-esteem comes most powerfully when we
are loved by others, by those who are tolerant and forgiving,
who are quick to praise and thank us for our good intentions
and best efforts. We seem to need a certain experience of
being so loved before we can begin to love. The communal
person provides this experience for the people he associates
with. And so, the best hope for the growth of altruism is in
the love of communal persons. Those who love enable others
to love simply by making love a credible reality. They are
the answer to the Utopian objection.

What looks at first like a poor, solitary hope for community thus turns out to have global potential in the end.
For those who meet communal persons have some ongoing
experience of being loved simply for being who they are, of
being praised and thanked, trusted and forgiven, and come
at last to believe in the reality of love and community. They
are then able to step out of their defensive self-primacy and
to love in return, thus becoming further centers of the contagion. There is no guarantee, of course, that anyone will begin
to love in return, for the choice to believe in love and to make
it one's life-goal is always a free one. But the possibility is
there, and along with it our world's best hope.

Peaceful hearts, like Mother Theresa's, will make their
sincere best efforts in the practical realm. They will make

mistakes, will fail out of weakness, will even be defeated by
circumstances beyond their control. But as long as their
mistakes are honest, their intentions pure, community will
persist and grow. Tolerance and compassion will spread, and
more and more people will find each other ready to forgive
and begin again. Even disastrous mistakes, colossal blunders,
frightening weaknesses and horrendous circumstances cannot
destroy the reality of community, once anyone takes it as a
motivating ideal. For just as we do not need to think of our
destination at every step of a journey, we need not explicitly think of community at each moment of every day, either.
Once having planned an itinerary, we follow it confidently,
knowing that we will reach our destination unless we deliberately change our intended direction. Communal identities
once assumed, communal motives once established, will persist unless they are deliberated revoked. And with them the
basic, inner reality of community will persist as well.

Contractual associations do not offer a similar hope, however. A solitary, self-centered individual cannot bring about
societies without the express cooperation of other solitary individuals. He must succeed in moving people closer together
in time and space if his contractual relationships are to have
any reality at all. He may be able to coerce the cooperation
of his fellows, but he cannot win them to his ideals through
his own credibility as a person. Indeed, he has no credibility.
Seeking rather to be loved than to love, willing to love only
when the benefits to himself outweigh the costs, he is absolutely dependent on the reciprocity of his fellows. And yet,
the only urgency he can give them for joining his company
comes from the rewards he can offer, rewards that outweigh
the costs of the association. In contractual associations, the
dynamics of credibility are lacking. An egoist is not transformed into a tolerant, forgiving person who is quick to praise
his associates, to thank them, to give them credit for their
good intentions. There are, indeed, no good intentions to
give credit for. He can only praise them for their outward
successes, and the praise redounds to their isolation. He can
only thank people for what benefits himself, since that is
what he seeks from his associations. He must be critical, in-
tolerant of mistakes and weaknesses, for if he tolerates these,
his enterprise fails. He is, in short, incredible.

Since he lacks credibility, the contagion by which one
loving person leads others to love does not happen in groupings which are mere associations. The psychological dynamics, by which love, praise and gratitude release people from

their fears, do not operate. Instead of building security and
self-esteem, in himself and in his associates, the contractual
lover reinforces suspicion, defensiveness, and anxious self-
absorption. He brings no one to believe in the reality of
love and community. Thus the failure to take community as
a real ideal has implications that are, finally, global. Instead
of community rippling outward from a multitude of credible
individuals, each self-centered individualist draws everything
toward his own incredible center. One mistake leads to another, one failure to another, until despair becomes a sickness
unto death. The sickness is the death of community itself,
and with it the death of human fulfillment.

Our options, then, are not between associations that we
find satisfying and enjoyable and those that displease us. The
question of community is a question of realization, in both
senses of that term. We first must realize community in the
ontological sense – we must make it humanly real, by appropriating it, in our altruistic loving Such love may not be
easy, or pleasant, or outwardly successful: it may indeed be
dark and painful. But the choice to love does make community happen. And eventually the healing light will come.
Then we will realize community in the second sense – we will
know, in a way that we have never known before, that it is
real. Its reality as an interior regime will dawn on us. We will
feel it in our bones. Contractual associations cannot realize
community in either of these ways. But once a group of mere
associates accepts community as a real ideal, making it the
motive for their praxis, they can play to each other's better
selves. That is, they can judge each other by their common
ideal rather than by their actual achievements. They will
enjoy moral, if not artistic, success.

Such playing to each other's better selves is no fantasy, no
wishful thinking. For our best, communal selves are – thanks
to the community of being into which we are born – our
true selves. Trust, tolerance, forgiveness are not contrived,
artificial, calculated attitudes. They are responses to what we
want each other to be. We play to what we want each other
to become by conscious choice, because we recognize what we
already are by our membership in the community of being.
Tolerance, trust, forgiveness and credit for good intentions
are solidly grounded in reality. Our tendency to appropriate
the community of being in altruistic love, no matter how
deeply buried and obscured by our practical failures, is our
deepest and truest tendency. Our egocentric, competitive
selves do not deserve the reality which our various contracts

bestow on them.[40]

It is a difficult, demanding, and life-long task to make our
motives altruistic. The conversion to altruism goes against
an ingrained selfishness that can be surprisingly fierce. And
the possibility of self-deception is a constant hazard. When
the Catholic bishops of the world met in Rome in 1980 to
discuss the status of the family in contemporary society, the
then Archbishop of Cincinnati, Joseph Bernardin, said that
the most important message for all of them to take back to
their people was the holiness of sexual intimacy. He then
added that the key to sexual intimacy is a couple's shared
effort to overcome their deep tendencies to self-deception.
He could have been speaking to all of us, about all forms
of genuine community. Sexual intimacy is one of the more
common ones, a uniquely dramatic and powerfully attractive
kind of community. But the one condition necessary for any
and all communities is still altruistic love, the tie that binds.
In order to achieve that love even for a moment, we have to
have a sincere desire for it, a pure intention to enact it in
praxis, and a sincere best effort in that direction. And part
of each step of the entire enterprise is a sincere best effort to
overcome our self-deception.

The final answer to the Utopian objection to community,
then, is that we really have no alternative. Altruistic love
may be difficult, complicated, hard to understand and harder
still to enact in praxis. But it is not Utopian. We could say
of it something similar to what Churchill said of democracy:
"Democracy," he said, "is the worst form of government that
there is – except all the others that have been tried." Appropriation of the community of being in altruistic love is
the worst way that there is for people to associate with each
other – except for all the others that have been tried, or even
thought of. And yet, because we have no alternative, we may
simply say, with the poet,

Be what you is,
because
If you be what you ain't,
then
You ain't what you is.

[40] The dynamics of the love by which we play to each other's better selves is
wonderfully described by Hans Urs von Balthazar in "The Freedom of the Subject,"
Cross Currents 12, Fall 1962, pp. 13-31. This article is translated from the German,
out of one of von Balthazar's major philosophical works (*Warheit*), by Gerald Farley.

EPILOGUE
A RETURN TO CASES

We have reached a point of return, a time to recall the cases with which this investigation began, and to answer the fundamental questions about community that those cases raise. The first case cited is, of course, Socrates – Socrates condemned of a capital crime and awaiting his conviction in a prison cell. Presented, by Crito, with a plan of escape, Socrates declines, with the explanation that an escape would violate and destroy the very laws which have been the source of his being. By his very choice to live in Athens for many years, and to establish a family there, he has made an agreement or compact with the laws. To violate that compact would be an injustice, an injustice which would contradict all his previous teachings. How could he, who has repeatedly taught the young men of the city that it is far worse to do evil than to suffer it, now perform an injustice in order to save his life? To do so would be to become, indeed, the corrupter of the young that he has been condemned as. Since his unjust sentence is procedurally correct, he has no appeal. His death is an injustice done to him by men, not by the laws. Out of loyalty to those laws, he will accept his death.

A casual reading of this dialogue can lead us to see Socrates as an adherent of social contract theory and even of legal positivism. He has made a compact with the laws of Athens, and those laws, which include procedures by which he is being brought to his death, are the only laws that there are. They cannot be evaluated in the light of some higher, natural law. But such a reading of the *Crito* would be wrong. The view of Socrates here is a profoundly communal one, quite opposed to the view that political society is an artifact, constructed by the arbitrary will of human beings who then make laws as they please. As the subsequent discussion in the *Phaedo* will make abundantly clear, the primary focus of the thought of Plato and Socrates is the search for unchanging, absolute, transcendent moral standards. Platonic Form Theory originates and persists as an inquiry into moral standards that can ground some sort of stable social and political life. These standards, which Socrates sees embodied in the laws of Athens, are really existing concrete entities which can make demands on us, including the final demand of giving up our lives. When Socrates chooses, then, to die rather than disobey the laws of his beloved Athens, he is showing, by

161

the ultimate test, the sincerity of his inquiry into the truth
about justice. Such sincerity is his entry into the community
of such inquirers. And he rightly decides that a life apart
from that community would not be worth living. He has
two quite different opportunities to save his life by departing
from community: he could propose exile as a legally acceptable alternative sentence, or he can follow Crito's plan and
go into exile without legal permission. Socrates declines both
options, and instead holds to the steady submission to truth,
a submission whose sincerity costs him his life, and thereby
prolongs his communal being until it is violently taken from
him.

If community is our appropriation of the community of
being in altruistic love, Socrates' decision makes perfect
sense. For therein lies his fulfillment as a person. In loving Crito well enough to reject his escape plan, which would
implicate both of them in an isolating, self-serving action,
Socrates appropriates the entire community of being. On
social contract terms, however, his decision would make no
sense whatsoever. The social contract, whose acceptance
binds us together into political and social groupings, aims at
preserving as much of our individualistic freedom as possible.
But death takes away every kind of fulfillment we might seek
for ourselves, for it takes away the self which is to be fulfilled.
Thus, when a given a hypothetical social contract – such as
Socrates' purported contractual acceptance of Athenian law
– becomes a threat to the self instead of its protector, logic
calls for a change in the compact. For Socrates, a departure from Athens on those terms would have been eminently
sensible. His self would live on, finding many fulfillments in
various useful and pleasant associations with his fellows in a
new and different social contract. But on communal terms,
such a life of exile won at the price of doing a severe injustice would be no life at all. The self that would enjoy such
apparent fulfillment would not really exist. Community on
such terms would be only apparent, not real. Socrates' argument thus rests on communal assumptions. What at first
blush appears to be an appeal to what moderns would call
a social contract is, rather, his appropriation of an inborn
communality. His acceptance of the laws of Athens is firmly
rooted in his sincere devotion to communal inquiry.

The relation of community to law is thus clear in
Socrates' case. Law is a set of guidelines that bind us, bind us
with a categorical moral obligation, to pursue certain behaviors and to avoid others. Law is a set of guidelines to loving,

and thus a road map to our only genuine way to exist, in community. To reject law, then, is to refuse to love, and thus to refuse our own existence as persons. Law prescribes what we must do because it describes what we are. Laws are not power-plays by which the strong control the weak. They are statements by which justice as fairness, fairness as the beauty of the way things are, finds itself symbolized in the words and institutions of authorities who know that objective state of affairs.

The second case, that of the troubled marriage of this author's aunt and godmother, raises questions about community on the smallest, most intimate scale – that of husband and wife. Once again an apparent contract is at issue – promises made long ago, when present circumstances could not have been foreseen. Marriage, like any other human association, can be either contractual or communal (or each in its turn, in a rhythm of peaks and valleys). The key question for a wife who finds herself abused by an alcoholic husband is, of course, one that contemporary culture practically shouts to all who promise fidelity "until death do us part." The question is about the value of suffering, about the nature of individual fulfillment and happiness, about the false equation of altruism, fidelity, and sacrifice with masochism and self-destruction. When a marriage turns out not to be what we bargained for, a contractual view of marriage calls for a renegotiation, a return to the bargaining table. If I enter a marriage for the sake of my fulfillment as an individual, for the pleasure and utility of my atomic ego, then surely I should depart from a union that does not meet those expectations. But communal thought can lead to another conclusion: granted the paradox of love, that a lover's existential fulfillment comes in union, through altruistic love, with a beloved's existence, then pain and suffering need not detract one iota from one's fulfillment as a person. Here we need only recall the dynamics of love within a community of being. To love is to wish for another his entire concrete well-being, for his sake. In exercising such love, a lover comes into union with that other's existence, and through that union appropriates the entire community of being. There is no greater human fulfillment. Aunt Catherine might have found a better life apart from her alcoholic husband – better in the sense of more pleasant, more useful for meeting many of her desires. But – granted that fidelity to him was the path to altruistic love – she would have lost her existential fulfillment in the act of separating. For to love one is to love all, and to fail to love one is to fail in loving all. Her options were to appropriate the community of being in its totality, or not to appropriate it at all.

The key here, of course, is deciding what, in the unique concrete situation, the demands of love might be. Surely there are marriages that ought to dissolve, spouses who ought to separate, because such a separation is precisely the good that one spouse must, out of love, will for the other. Whether separation is such a good or not will vary with circumstances, and knowing whether it is is surely one of the most difficult tasks that many will face in their entire lives. An obvious example would be an abusive drinking habit which was reasonably sure to continue. It is no act of love for a wife to permit a husband to abuse her. Such permission violates his welfare as a person, and love might well demand that she save him from his own self-destruction by departing from his bed and board. But in the present case, the circumstances were not so hopeless. This particular wife answered all the pleas, from relatives and friends, that she divorce her husband for her own sake with a steady altruism that was also quite realistic about their future together: "No," she would say, "I want to give him a chance to change." She was no collaborator in his self-destruction, then, but a lover demanding his reform, for his sake. As it turned out, her expectations were quite reasonable, her alcoholic husband reformed, and their intimacy became deeply joyous as well as existential. And no perceptible harm came to children or grandchildren from a marriage which, despite some difficult years, lasted as long as both lived – over thirty years.

Our third case has been much in the news for several years, having become a typical focus of discussion in medical ethics. Elizabeth Bouvia, a victim of cerebral palsy now in her early thirties, is expected to be an invalid all her life. Her life expectancy is normal, her health otherwise good, and her mind is clear and mature. She is able to converse and to move about in a wheelchair. Her case came to national attention when she sought hospital-assisted suicide. Convinced that her life was without meaning, and wishing it to end it by starvation, she asked for medical care in a hospital during the slow process of dying. The hospital refused, and Elizabeth Bouvia sued in court to force their compliance, but failed. At last report, she was seeking other avenues of support. Her story raises basic, and increasingly common, questions about medical care and life support, about who should live and who should die, about the meaning of human life – as

medical professionals often put it, about the quality of life.
A view of community as the way to human fulfillment can
cast important light on these and other current problems in
medical ethics.

In considering this particular "quality of life" case, we
must bring the contemporary view of human fulfillment, in
our culture, into confrontation with the first and most important conclusion drawn about community in the present
study. Put briefly and clearly, in Aristotle's terms, friendship consists more in loving than in being loved. It is love,
and love alone, that brings one person into community with
another and, in and through that other, with the entire community of being. One's total fulfillment as a person, then,
can be complete in a momentary, entirely interior action –
the choice to identify the well-being of another as one's own,
to wish his existence for his sake. Such love can surely be
exercised without any exterior action at all. Contemporary
cultural values locate fulfillment, meaning, and a high quality of life in such externals as the ability to move around, to
work, to make a contribution to society by earning one's way
and paying one's taxes. Old people are scorned as no longer
"pulling their weight in the boat." Mothers who choose to
accept welfare instead of jobs so that they can stay home to
care for their children are condemned for not doing anything
socially useful. It is no wonder, then, that an invalid might
begin to feel invalid as a person.

Elizabeth Bouvia carries in her own hands, however, the
meaning of her life and the hope of her own fulfillment as a
person. For she is perfectly able to love, and even to express
love in that wonderful set of externalizing symbols that make
up our language. She can, quite simply, affirm her own existence, in its own right, and that of the people around her. In
so doing, she will appropriate the entire community of being.
Her personal fulfillment will then be complete – more complete than if she were mobile and self-supporting, living for
egocentric motives, as many of her healthy associates may
well be. She can, with a loving heart, accept and cooperate
with the care that she needs to receive from others. She can
welcome their care as their way of finding their fulfillment
through the exercise of altruistic love for her. For if friendship consists rather in loving than in being loved, one whose
physical circumstances call for receiving a great deal of loving
care, over the length of a life, can easily turn the receiving of
love into its giving. Indeed, needy as we all are of constant
attention and concern from our fellows, we can receive that

attention and concern in two different ways. We can seek, in
Auden's words, "not love universal, but to be loved alone."
In that search to be loved, the healthiest, most mobile and
productive person among us can pervert the entire meaning
of our lives. Invalids, on the other hand – even those who, unlike Elizabeth Bouvia, are not even able to speak – can enjoy
the highest possible quality of life as they lovingly affirm the
existence of their fellows, thus appropriating the entire community of being in altruistic love. We must conclude that in
several other current court cases in the United States, physicians will have the best of it, morally, even if not legally. In
the cases in question, families are suing for the removal of
feeding tubes from relatives who are not dying and not co-
matose – people who are bedridden but conscious, alert, and
able to communicate through gestures and eye contact. Such
invalids may well be living lives richer in human fulfillment
and meaning than are their healthy, wealthy and mobile crit-
ics. Their physicians are fighting to keep them alive.

Our fourth case, that of Officer Thomas Buntrock, is a
paradigm of self-sacrifice. It also raises some important questions about the meaning of life, about moral goodness, and
about the relation of the individual to society – all questions that are answered quite differently when approached
with contractual and with communal assumptions. Officer
Buntrock and his fellow officers were chasing an armed bank
robber, who took a young father and his 2-year old daugh-
ter hostage. Officer Buntrock put down his gun and asked
the gunman to release the baby and take him hostage in her
place. The robber agreed, the exchange was made, and the
gunman was sufficiently distracted that the father was able
to escape as well. A few minutes later, multiple shots flew
between the robber and the police. The robber and Officer
Buntrock were both killed by policemen's bullets. The small
town later recognized Buntrock as a hero and erected a public statue in his honor. What are we to make of someone's
voluntarily giving up his life in such a situation?

The principles on which we answer such a question will
make a great difference in the conclusion which we reach.
On the basis of contractual principles, Officer Buntrock was
a fool. His generous impulse would be admired, of course.
But it would be taken as precisely that, an impulse – a hasty
decision, made in the heat of emotion, out of strong pity for
an innocent child, perhaps, or out of the false grandeur of a
stereotypical masculinity. But what would a rational analysis
make of that impulse? Here, Crito's plea to Socrates seems to

the point. Officer Buntrock had children of his own, children now deprived of their father. The plight of the child hostage was in no way his fault, and so, he had no obligation to rectify it. In terms of the social contract, he and the child had equal rights to life, neither life being more valuable than the other. Indeed, a possible calculus might see his life as of greater worth, given his place in his family and the society in which he lived. True, once having accepted a policeman's role, he has contracted to risk his life in order to save the lives of innocent citizens threatened by criminal violence. But what about such a contract in the first place? Officer Buntrock was not, prior to offering himself as a hostage, risking his life in order to save an innocent fellow-citizen – at least, not so immediately, and so surely, as he did by becoming hostage himself. A utilitarian or hedonistic calculus, carefully figuring the odds, could lead one to undertake a career in public safety. In ordinary police work, fire protection, and military life steps are taken to make the odds of losing one's life in the line of duty as favorable as possible. Policies and procedures are designed to minimize risks. No such contract would require anyone to substitute for a hostage.

In light of all these considerations, Officer Buntrock's action turns out to be impulsive, foolish, a needless loss of life. No one would have blamed him had he decided not to offer himself as a hostage. Since he may have protected his life in a perfectly rational way, he might have lived on to find meaning and fulfillment as a person. As it was, he lost meaning and fulfillment when he lost his life. A dead man no longer exercises his individual freedom in the pursuit of a happiness that he defines for himself, in various negotiations – with wife and family, friends and society – negotiations pertaining to the freedom and rights of others seeking their happiness as they see fit. Self-fulfillment governed by contractual principles founders on the rock of self-sacrifice.

Communal principles, however, lead to a different conclusion. Here, we can see Officer Buntrock as a member of the community of being, individually limited but able to transcend himself in altruistic love. Granted that his becoming a substitute hostage was a decision motivated by altruistic love – an affirmation of the child's existence for the child's sake – the officer expanded his own being by coming into possession of the being of the child he loved. Since her being is the actuation of everything else about her, Officer Buntrock was in communion with the totality of the child's entire life. Further, given her membership in the community of being,

her ties to all other beings in and through the omnipresence
of the one God, he appropriated, in that one momentary act,
the entire community of being. He thus came into communion with the totality of the lives of his own children as well
– even though he was momentarily to lose his association
with them in time and space. Office Buntrock thus gained
an enormous fulfillment for himself, an existential fulfillment
as great as any could be. Seen from another angle, had he
refused, out of cowardice or selfishness, to act out his generous impulse, he might well have saved his life at the cost
of his personal fulfillment. He might have lived on for many
years in the company of his wife and children, his friends and
fellow citizens, thus enjoying countless utilitarian and hedonistic benefits. But the price for those benefits would have
been precisely his loss of existential fulfillment in community,
his own fullness of existence as a person. Given an ongoing
selfish motivation, he would not have been in communion
with his family or with anyone else, even if he enjoyed their
space-time closeness and even intimacy.

Finally, we come to Mother Theresa of Calcutta, a global
hero of altruistic love whom millions admire but few feel com-
pelled to imitate. Time was when she was an adolescent girl,
looking ahead to a life full of promise, trying to decide what
sort of person to become. What about the decision that led
her to spend her days rescuing poor, unknown dying people
from dying alone? Of course, she is meeting the needs of
her fellow human beings in an apparent enactment of altruistic love. But the needs that she meets seem so minimal.
Is it really worth someone's entire life to ease the deaths of
unknown, unimportant people who may not even thank her?
She doesn't save lives, after all. She only washes dirty bodies,
gives the simplest, plainest food to those who can swallow,
holds the hands of strangers as they take their last breaths.
A nice touch, perhaps, but something to devote one's life to?

Once again, communal and contractual premises will lead
us to opposite conclusions. For those who accept the communal nature of human beings, thus locating our personal
fulfillment in our appropriating the community of being in
altruistic love, Mother Theresa's work is, indeed, worth the
dedication of her life. It is, in fact, her fulfillment as a person, a fulfillment as magnificent as any she might have sought
anywhere else. The picture that appeared on the front pages
of newspapers all over the world on the occasion of her Nobel Peace Prize depicts community in all its glory: Mother
Theresa was shown cradling an emaciated baby in her arms.

The caption told us why Mother Theresa does what she does: "This baby," she explained, "is starving, and there is nothing we can do to save its life. It will be dead in a short while. But at least it will know the touch of human love before it dies." Who knows how far that touch might extend? The power of love flowing out of a single credible person is often enough to change another's whole life. Perhaps that dying child was enabled to love for just a moment, thus finding its entire fulfillment as a person. Probably many of the adults whom Mother Theresa cares for are brought to a realization of love that turns their entire lives around in their last moments.

To imagine that Mother Theresa is some sort of closet egoist or masochist seems absurd on the face of it, but such an image is needed if we are to value her work on the basis of contractual principles. A hedonistic or utilitarian calculus on her part is well nigh incredible, but let us make the hypothesis nonetheless. Suppose Mother Theresa sees herself as an individual ego, a center of rights and the freedom to pursue them, a woman who has the right to do whatever she wants with her own body. She is free, then, to define her happiness, to claim it, and seek it freely, subject only to restraints that come about when her freedom conflicts with someone else's. Then the conflict is resolved through negotiations in which she and her competitors all give up some of their freedom in order to preserve the rest. They collaborate in each other's search for individual satisfaction, each seeking happiness as he or she sees fit, for his or her own sake. In such a view, Mother Theresa seems rather harmless and may be left to do her own thing. To each his own, so long as nobody gets hurt. Masochistic, perhaps – but masochism brings its own twisted pleasure. Poverty, chastity and obedience are fine for some people. Wealth and pleasure and unrestrained egoism are someone else's preferences. And so, live and let live. As the song has it, "Whatever gets you through the night."

These five cases, then, raise many of the important questions that a philosophy of community must grapple with. In some ways, they are unusual. Few of us face Socrates' situation, condemned to death by men who misuse the laws that we revere. Many marriages and families flourish without the ravages of alcoholism challenging the resources of love, pushing them nearly to the breaking point. Millions live out their lives in good health and mobility, never facing the challenge of finding a meaningful way to live in a wheelchair or on a paralytic's bed. Few indeed are called to offer themselves as hostages in place of innocent children. And Mother Theresa's order, while it is attracting more novices every day, may never become the world's largest organization. And yet, these five individuals have something to tell the rest of us as we live our more ordinary lives, seeking our human fulfillment in ordinary work and family life, in ordinary cultural and social and political life. What they show us is the life and death choice with which every human being is faced in every daily decision about how to associate with his fellow humans. That choice is, quite simply, whether or not to love, whether to seek each other's good for each other's sake, or whether to seek our own good for our own sake.

The only answer to that question became dramatically clear at the ceremony at which Mother Theresa accepted the Nobel Peace Prize. Before an audience of notables from all over the world, people whose concern was the peace of the world, her frail arms beckoned everyone to stand, and to bow their heads in prayer. The prayer in which she led them was the Prayer for Peace attributed to St. Francis – the prayer which says, in part,

Grant that I may not so much seek
  To be consoled as to console,
  To be understood as to understand,
  To be loved as to love;
For it is in giving that we receive,
It is in pardoning that we are pardoned,
And it is in dying that we are born to eternal life.

BIBLIOGRAPHY

Auden, W. H. "September 1, 1939," *The Collected Poetry of W. H. Auden.* New York: Random House, 1965.

Ashmore, Jr., Robert B. "Ewing on 'Higher' Egoism," *The New Scholasticism.* Autumn 1977, pp. 513-523.

Bellah, Robert, Richard Madsen, William Sullivan, Ann Swidler, and Steven Tipton. *Habits of the Heart: Individualism and Commitment in American Life.* Berkeley: University of California Press, 1985.

Constable, Giles. *Religious Life and Thought, 11th and 12th Centuries.* London: Variorum Reprints, 1979.

Cooper, John M. "Aristotle on the Forms of Friendship," *Review of Metaphysics.* June 1977, pp. 618-648.

Cooper, John M. "Friendship and the Good in Aristotle," *The Philosophical Review.* July, 1977, pp. 290-315.

Cornford, Francis Macdonald. *Plato and Parmenides: Parmenides' Way of Truth and Plato's Parmenides.* London: Routledge, 1951.

Davitt, Thomas E. *The Basic Values in Law.* Milwaukee: Marquette University Press, 1978.

Dick, Oliver Lawson, ed. *Aubreys' Brief Lives.* London: Secker and Warburg, 1949.

Eliot, T. S. and Hoellering, George. *The Film of Murder in the Cathedral.* New York: Harcourt, Brace and Company, 1935.

Hammarskjold, Dag. *Markings.* Translated by Leif Sjoberg and W. H. Auden. New York: Alfred A. Knopf, 1966.

Johann, Robert O. *The Meaning of Love.* Glen Rock, NJ: Paulist Press, 1966.

Kirkpatrick, Frank G. *Community, A Trinity of Models.* Washington, D.C.: Georgetown University Press, 1986.

Kolakowski Leszek. *Religion.* London: Oxford University Press, 1982.

Leakey, Richard E. and Roger Lewin. *Origins: What New Discoveries Reveal About the Emergence of Our Species and Its Possible Future.* New York: E. P. Dutton, 1977.

Macmurray, John. *Persons in Relation.* Atlantic Highlands: Humanities Press, 1979.

McKeon, Richard. *The Basic Works of Aristotle.* New York: Random House, 1941.

Mouroux, Jean. *The Meaning of Man.* Garden City: Doubleday and Co., Inc., 1961.

Nef, John. "Is the Intellectual Life an End in Itself?" *The Review of Politics, XXIV*, 1962, pp.3-18.

Nisbet, Robert A. *Quest for Community.* London: Oxford University Press, 1969.

Rawls, John. *A Theory of Justice.* Cambridge: Harvard University Press, 1971.

Roth, Robert, S.J. *Person and Community: A Philosophical Exploration.* New York: Fordham University Press, 1975.

Rousseau, Edward L. "Dialogue and the Atheist." *Continuum* Autumn 1965, pp. 398-399.

Rousseau, Mary F. "Problems of Dialog: Invincible Ignorance." *Listening,* 5:Winter, 1970, pp. 67-71.

Rousseau, Mary F. "Community: Elusive Unity, Indeed." *The New Scholasticism,* 60, 3, Summer 1986, pp. 356-365.

Schell, Jonathan. *The Fate of the Earth.* New York: Alfred A. Knopf, 1982.

Schmitz, Kenneth L. "Community, Elusive Unity," *Review of Metaphysics,* 37. 1983, pp.243-264.

Tierney, Brian. *Church Law and Constitutional Thought in the Middle Ages.* London: Variorum Reprints, 1979.

Tinder, Glenn. "The Secular City." *The New Republic.* August 16 and 23, 1982.

Tinder, Glenn. *Community: Reflections on a Tragic Ideal.* Baton Rouge: Louisiana State University Press, 1980.

Tonniës, Ferdinand. *Community and Society.* New York: Harper Brothers, 1957.

von Balthazar, Hans Urs. "The Freedom of the Subject." *Cross Currents,* Fall 1962, pp. 13-31. Translated by Gerald Farley.

Wojtyla, Karol. *The Acting Person.* Dordrecht, Holland:
    D. Reidel Publishing Company, 1979. Translated by
    Andrzej Potocki.